I0155462

THE CITYBOT'S
LIBRARY

ESSAYS ON THE TRANSFORMERS

THE CITYBOT'S
LIBRARY

ESSAYS ON THE TRANSFORMERS

JULIAN DARIUS

The Citybot's Library: Essays on the Transformers
by Julian Darius

Copyright © 2008, 2012, 2013, 2014, 2024 Julian Darius.

First edition, July 2024, ISBN 978-1-940589-35-0.

All rights reserved by the author. Except for brief excerpts used for review or scholarly purposes, no part of this book may be reproduced in any manner whatsoever, including electronic, without express written consent of the author.

Several of the essays in this volume have previously appeared on Sequart Organization's website. One also appeared on the website of Literary Escort Services.

Cover by Julian Darius. Book design by Julian Darius.

Published by Sequart Organization. For more information about this or other titles, visit Sequart.org/books.

Table of Contents

The Transformers are Stupid!: Why I Love the Transformers

In Autobot City, there is a library, filled with obscure tomes. Some are from Cybertron's past, dusty and rarely consulted — religious predictions and screeds, long discounted and forgotten, written by robotic prophets and vehicular madmen. Other volumes come from various parallel universes the Autobots have contacted, from worlds vastly different from the one in which this city sits. In the library's branching corridors, there are even comics and video recordings from worlds in which the whole Cybertronian species never existed and therefore had to be dreamed up — worlds where the Cybertronian war never spilled onto thousands of worlds, devastating their populations, where Earth was spared decades of urban devastation and humans were permitted to kill each other instead.

No one uses the library anymore... except Perceptor. He knows the others think him high-strung and overly serious, but he thinks they're too superficial, too focused on racing and fighting and play-fighting. But when he's done with his duties for the day, analyzing the city's vast network of energy flows to ensure maximal efficiency, he turns to the library to relax. Since no one uses it, he's become its *de facto* curator, reorganizing it according to his own schema. Sometimes, he sinks into the chair he's placed in the library, which faces the window with its view of the city's other towers, sheets of metal and light rising into the heavens, backdropped against the green plain and the mountains rising beyond. Other times, like today, he transforms into telescope mode and examines the pages that way, employing a non-sentient page-turner. It is the closest thing he has to meditation.

* * *

Let's be honest: the Transformers are stupid. At their core, they're based on the simplest of ideas: getting two toys in one, a robot who turns into a vehicle (or weapon) of some sort. That's how the original toy line evolved, as Hasbro worked with Japanese company Takara to fuse multiple lines, plus a few odds and ends, into a single toy line. That's why the original G1 toys featured both regular cars that scaled with Optimus Prime and mini-cars, like Bumblebee, who were actually from a separate line of toys intended to be 1:1 scale – they were *toy cars*, which is why they look a little deformed, that turned into tiny robots. In the same way, 1:1 scale characters like Megatron, who turned into a gun humans could hold, and Soundwave, who turned into a micro-cassette player, were put on the same team with robots who turned into jets that were about the same size. Because the Transformers line explicitly wasn't a line of mechs, controlled by human pilots, those pilots would be removed from the Dinobot and the Insecticon toys, although they still had the cockpits. The same could be said of Optimus Prime's trailer. The result was a messy hodgepodge of different toys with different scales.

Some of their robot modes were so ugly that the animation models created *to sell the toys* simply ignored what the toys actually looked like and redesigned whole parts of them. This included both factions' leaders: both the holes in Optimus Prime's sides left by his arms and the gun trigger left in Megatron's crotch were redesigned. Imagine if Bumblebee's arms had been kept as weird little poles that rotated at different points along his chest! And that's not even considering Jetfire, who was a Macross jet in the actual toy but who was redesigned and renamed Skyfire in the cartoon because the cartoon would also air in Japan, where someone else had that toy's license. Faced with toys of totally different scales, the fiction simply ignored this, having characters like Megatron and Soundwave *grow* as they transformed, so they could be about the right size in robot mode. Numerous absurd errors, of the same Transformers depicted at vastly different sizes, sometimes riding in each other or even the same size as humans, would be incredibly common for *years*.

None of this should have worked. It was, to be charitable, a mess.

The line had no origin story, no mythology. It fell to Marvel Comics to come up with this and to name the characters. The Transformers could have been the creation of some secret human program, some Doc Brown sort of character. But that would have minimalized them, subjected them to human control. And so instead, the problem of how giant transforming robots got to Earth was solved with the same slight of hand that Jerry Siegel and Joe Shuster used to explain their super-powered Superman, all those years ago: they were aliens! Because anything can come from outer space.

And so was created Cybertron and its inhabitants' civil war. Of course, this captivating solution created new problems: who had created these robots? Why did they have space for drivers, even on Cybertron, if they didn't live among humanoids?

To justify why they had human alt modes, we were told the Transformers were "robots in disguise." That might've worked for the first batch of toys, but you knew it was the thinnest of justifications because there was no way robotic dinosaurs and giant robotic insects were designed for the purpose of laying low. Later, the character Cosmos turned into a flying saucer!

None of this makes sense, really. But it was full of cool ideas. In the 1980s, robots that turned into vehicles and fought each other sold themselves. And seriously, who doesn't love robotic dinosaurs? Perhaps more than any other franchise, Transformers is based around starting with cool ideas and coming up with explanations afterwards.

But unlike most other franchises, the superficial justifications *worked*. The Transformers didn't wave a wand and get these only partly satisfying justifications out of the way. No, they *invested* in them, owning their stupid ideas and working them until they resonated and felt like a mythology. Cybertron had a mystique all to itself, and even in those early stories, any glimpse of Cybertron was a real treat. Superman works that same way, but the sooner we forget about the explanations for most franchises, the better. It's usually best not to think too hard about why Thanos is doing what he's doing, or what else Tony Stark or Mr. Fantastic could be doing with their inventions. But with the Transformers, it's hard not to want more exploration, more explanations.

Even the absurd way that the toy line was assembled wound up working to its advantage. Having different size toys at very different price points let kids on a budget buy in, while still craving that expensive Optimus Prime or Omega Supreme figure. In a time when there were still neighborhoods with kids who played with toys together, those kids would pool their resources, getting to experience the characters they couldn't afford. It's similar to the principle of rarity among collectable cards: when the cards are each as common as each other (a strategy initially taken by the rival line of transforming robots, the Go-Bots), there's less of a sense of the hunt, of having to choose exactly which items one wants in one's collection, and of the excitement of seeing something rare in someone else's hands.

And the Transformers kept reinventing themselves, with combiners, female Transformers, the futuristic vehicles introduced with the animated movie, and humanoids who turned into the robots' heads and guns and engines. And all along the way, instead of running away from those silly explanations, the fiction built a mythology around them: Megatron being a lowly gladiator, Orion Pax becoming Optimus Prime, ancient Autobots like Alpha Trion, secrets like Vector Sigma buried within Cybertron, the ghost of Starscream, the Matrix of Leadership, the ancient threat of Unicron, rival space factions like the Quintessons, and Primus in the comics. The Autobot leaders struggled with confidence, and characters were occasionally allowed to evolve and switch sides. Like Cybertron and the concept of "robots in disguise," some of these new elements didn't make sense either: how did gender work in robots? Tell me again how humanoids fold up into heads or guns or engines and stay in those stress positions for days? But even when the Transformers franchise was *stupid*, it was shot full of cool ideas that made you *want* a better explanation.

Ultimately, this penchant for gimmicks and reinvention ran dry. The toys introduced micromasters, tiny toys intended to chase the popularity of Micro Machines but which only emphasized the scale problem and never got much of an explanation in the fiction. Then came action masters, distinguished by *not transforming*.

By then, there was no fiction to even offer an explanation. Their cartoon was cancelled (except in Japan). The American comic book was cancelled after 80 issues. The toy line petered out, having achieved its highest point with the massive Fortress Maximus, which stood nearly two feet tall in robot mode and was priced at $100 in 1987. In a time when most successful toy lines only lasted a couple years, Transformers seemed destined to go the way of Super Powers, Masters of the Universe, Voltron, Thundercats, M.A.S.K., and G.I. Joe. In fact, any betting person would have been smart to lay odds on G.I. Joe being the franchise with more life in it: having started earlier than the Transformers, it was *already* a revival of an older toy line and had, in its 1980s incarnation, lasted longer than the Transformers – as a toy line, as a cartoon, *and* as a comic – although it also petered out, beset by gimmicks that deviated too far from the core concept.

In late 1992, the Transformers returned with Generations 2, which consisted mostly of recolored old toys along with a few new molds; old cartoons with new, annoying framing sequences; and a new comic book that was so doomed to failure that its writer, Simon Furman, named its new big bad "Gee, axe us" – or Jhiaxus. Although the line lasted until 1995, it wasn't very popular.

Then, in 1996, came Beast Wars, which reimagined the Transformers as turning into organic animals and which featured an early computer-generated cartoon show. Although largely eschewed by fans of the original line, now given the retronym Generation 1 (or G1), Beast Wars would be a tremendous success with a new generation, taking its focus on characterization to new levels and eventually tying into G1 continuity, continuing the mythos.

From then on, the Transformers cartoons essentially continued uninterrupted. Beast Wars shifted towards mechanical animals, and then vehicles returned. After a full reboot with 2001's Robots in Disguise, which has since fallen into obscurity, a trilogy of Japanese cartoons were imported to the U.S. market, where their reception was more than a bit lukewarm. Then came the tremendously successful 2007 live-action movie – something unthinkable to old-school fans. From then on, the franchise has never taken a break, going from one cartoon reboot to the next, alongside the live-action movies and multiple lines of toys.

Not to mention comics. In fact, it was comics that demonstrated the astounding continued popularity of Generation 1. When Dreamwave began publishing Transformers comics, it did so with a reimagining of Generation 1. Despite no one wanting the license to make Transformers comics since Generation 2, the first Dreamwave issue was the top-selling comic that month, and subsequent issues would continue to rank highly, beating top-tier Marvel and DC names like Spider-Man, the X-Men, Batman, and Superman. Dreamwave's comics would even explore Cybertron's backstory in a side series, subtitled *The War Within*. When the license moved to IDW in 2005, it began an unbroken new continuity, also based on Generation 1, that would last 14 years and would introduce new characters and new depth to old characters. When the license moved to Skybound in 2023, the first issue again topped the charts.

And then there's the video games, most prominently 2010's amazing *War for Cybertron* and its 2012 sequel, *Fall of Cybertron*, which combined to serve as a prequel to the Transformers coming to Earth.

As a kid, I had several Transformers toys, including Optimus Prime, Blaster, and several others. But I had just as many Super Powers and M.A.S.K. toys — and far more Masters of the Universe toys, including Castle Grayskull and Skull Mountain. But I felt I outgrew He-Man, and the line that ended up winning was G.I. Joe — which my parents, traumatized by the Vietnam draft, had initially forbidden me to own. Although I never owned the U.S.S. Flagg, I had several big G.I. Joe vehicles I adored. While I never fell out of love with the animated Transformers movie, I owned few Transformers toys after 1987. By the early 1990s, I eagerly purchased the Generation 2 comic, but it was already an exercise in nostalgia: I had soured on the silliness of late Generation 1 toys and comics, I never purchased any Generation 2 toys, and the cartoon show only reminded me of how badly I felt the franchise had been bungled. I didn't hate Beast Wars, but it wasn't the Transformers I knew and loved. While I gobbled up the Dreamwave comics, I tried the cartoon reboots of the early 2000s, but they were too much for kids. And I never bought any of the toys, despite examining a few; they were too flawed and too expensive for me, especially since I no longer collected toys, outside of an rare figure or two, whimsically purchased for my desk.

It wasn't until I saw imported Binaltech toys, while living in Hawaii, that I truly felt tempted again. Although they were expensive, I eventually bought a couple, then started buying toys for the 2007 movie. I had a bit of a mental breakdown in 2008, when I finished my French M.A. and had nothing but my dissertation left for my English Ph.D. – culminating in me moving back to live with my parents, late in the year, while I finished my dissertation. My Transformers toys sat in big boxes, shipped from Hawaii, too painful for me to open or even check that they were all there.

I certainly saw Hasbro's move into new, better molds of classic characters, but I didn't bite until the 2010 "Battle in Space" set, featuring new, objectively better molds of Hot Rod and Cyclonus, from my beloved animated movie, along with a comic telling a new side story set during the movie. Even in 1986, I'd rejected the toys based on the movie for being too simplistic and too different from the characters' on-screen versions. Now, I saw that technology and corporate will was catching up with the versions of the toys that I wanted. Still, I resisted getting back into toys. But by 2014, I surrendered, blown away by new, better versions of Devastator and Metroplex. I waded into the expensive Masterpiece line and into third-party (unlicensed) Transformers, often staring at them in awe. As of this writing, I've never recovered.

I've often marveled at how much I love the Transformers, especially given how surprising this would have been to me as a child. A huge part of this is the sheer amount of amazing toys, not to mention new stories, whether in comics or in movies, that I care about. We've seen a lot of revivals of franchises originating in the 1980s, but there can be no doubt that the Transformers are the clear winner.

That said, I'll be the first to acknowledge that it's a wildly inconsistent franchise. I can point to great episodes from various cartoon shows and great runs in the comics, but there are plenty of duds along the way – or series that might be fine, but are aimed too young for me to be able to enjoy or even properly evaluate. I'll defend half the movies, although I'll acknowledge they have flaws – and that the other half of the movies are truly *bad*, in some shocking ways, although I'll defend a few characters or scenes.

At their worst, the underlying stupidity of the Transformers shines through: why don't they just scan and become a more powerful vehicle again? Could we at least get an explanation for how combiners work, or how Headmasters work, or all these new factions and gimmicks that get jammed into some of the movies?

But at their best, the Transformers is a set of amazing ideas – a *city* or a *planet...* or a kaiju that transforms into a robot! – that compel us to seek explanations, and those explanations *enhance* our sense of wonder, rather than diffuse it. How do you square organic and robotic animals with the idea of disguise? Why are the Decepticons military vehicles and the Autobots cars, and how do the Transformers understand this divide, if their biology is truly their destiny? Who created the Transformers, or how did they evolve? Do the Transformers have religion? How do we understand gender among robotic life? Is it fluid? If there are heterosexual Transformers relationships, are there homosexual ones? What's it like to live in a sentient city? Do the Transformers shift size as they transform, perhaps by accessing another dimension, or is this simply a mistake we should attempt to rectify in the next reboot? What's it like being part of a combining team that's lost a member and can't combine? How do you understand yourself, if you literally turn into a weapon, but you've renounced violence? How do we judge a non-organic, quasi-immortal species that has characters we look up to and love but that has also colonized planets and spread devastation to other worlds, including Earth?

I've thought about these things far too much, and I have my own preferred answers to these questions. There are a million stories I want to read. And these answers, like Cybertron itself, lead to more questions and more possibilities. Their answers can evoke a sense of intellectual wonder, even while the robotic action triggers the release of adrenaline, the design work evokes an aesthetic passion, and the characters themselves can make you laugh and cry.

To the extent that I'm able to answer why I've kept my love of the Transformers, while my love of other franchises has diminished, I think a big part of the answer is that I've mellowed as I've gotten older. I was a very serious young man. A certain kind of story – a very serious kind – takes a single idea and explores its implications. *Watchmen* fits this mold, as does most "high" literature. Some fiction is filled with cool ideas, but doesn't seem to care about explaining them, and I wind up feeling like the fiction doesn't care about its own story, much less my time and thought. With the Transformers, the crazy idea comes first: we got this giant kaiju Decepticon we're trying to sell! But then they try to explain it, to turn that crazy idea into a story that – ideally – makes sense and opens up new possibilities and implications. It's like an intellectual puzzle. It doesn't always work, and I might always want more sense, more thoughtfulness, more implications. But it's a wonderful model for telling stories and for building a mythos.

And even the worst Transformers stories are interesting enough, or contain a cool enough idea or explanation for that idea, that I imagine how it might be done better and want to read the next reboot's attempt.

* * *

An alarm sounds, awakening Perceptor from his meditation. He instinctively transforms into robot mode, but it's already too late. He can hear the groan of skyscrapers folding, of plazas sliding open to swallow them, of a thousand vast metal plates grinding against a thousand other vast metal plates.

The walls constrict and open up. Books tumble from the shelves. Perceptor catches those he can, knowing it's useless. Soon, the entire room turns on its side, sending books cascading everywhere. Perceptor lies on bookcases, now on the floor, buried in obscure and forgotten tomes.

He gets to his feet. His chair lies overturned among hundreds of books. Above him, the bookcases on the ceiling are empty now, though their dust still drifts down through the library. On the side walls, bookcases sit sideways, their rows of contents turned into columns, lying violently asunder. Through the window, there are no more metal skyscrapers – there is only the green field far below and those distant mountains, now at eye level.

He hates to leave the library in such a state, but Perceptor knows he must get to the control room as soon as possible, to discover what crisis could possibly send the citybot into robot mode. Is Trypticon attacking? Is some Decepticon spaceship? Has there been a warning from Moonbase Two? He hopes Grimlock hasn't hit the button that forces a transformation... again.

It'll be a hard climb to the control room. The doors are designed to work in either mode, but he'll have to duck through them when they're sideways, then climb the ladders that run along the former ceilings of room after room. It could take hours, so it's best to get started.

Doing his best not to step on too many books, Perceptor makes it to the door, which opens automatically. A few books spill out, tumbling story after story down the hallway turned into a tall vertical shaft. Perceptor takes hold of the ladder, which used to run along the top of the hallway, and swings out of the library. He begins to climb.

Beneath him, a book tumbles into a horizontal door. Inside lives one of the humans who make Autobot City their home, now upturned. Thinking there was a knock at the door and an Autobot might be rescuing him, the human inside verbally orders the door to open. It slides to one side, revealing only the vast vertical shaft above him. Then a book tumbles into the room, lying upside-down on the floor.

The human picks it up and looks at the cover.

Its title is *The Citybot's Library*.

That human is you. Well, a *version* of you, anyway.

You begin to read.[*]

---

[*] This introduction is new to this volume.

Why "Man of Iron" May Be the Best Transformers Story Ever Told

When *Transformers* debuted from Marvel Comics in the U.S., it was originally a bimonthly four-issue mini-series, but it was so successful that it got extended. After a three-month pause between issues #4 (Mar 1985) and #5 (June 1985), the title continued monthly.

Meanwhile, Marvel's U.K. imprint brought out a British version of the title. In the U.K., comics have traditionally been weekly anthology titles. Initially, the U.K. version of the Transformers comic was biweekly and published mostly in black-and-white. It reprinted the U.S. stories, splitting each U.S. issue into two halves, so that each U.S. story would run over two U.K. issues. The first eight U.K. issues thus reprinted the first four U.S. issues.

After this, the U.K. series would have to generate new content, exclusive to the U.K. The British series wouldn't begin reprinting U.S. issue #5 until U.K. issue #22, meaning that the first eight reprint issues were followed by *13 issues* featuring new material unique to the U.K. These 13 issues were divided into three separate stories: "Man of Iron" (U.K. #9-12), "The Enemy Within!" (U.K. #13-17), and "Raiders of the Last Ark" (#18-21).

Because the U.S. mini-series ended with a cliffhanger, in which almost all the Autobots were defeated, these three British serials had to be set *during* the first four U.S. issues. Exactly when they occur isn't always clear.

This is especially true of the first U.K. story, "Man of Iron." Like the first U.S. issue, it featured illustrations that hewed closely to the toys, thus departing from how many characters would eventually be depicted. This situation would persist – although it would gradually improve – throughout this first batch of new U.K. stories. "Man of Iron" also departed from established Transformers lore in several key respects, which we'll explore later.

In retrospect, "Man of Iron" was very much an orphan. "The

Enemy Within!" was the first U.K. story written by Simon Furman, who would go on to write the vast majority of the new U.K. stories. Although "The Enemy Within!" loosely occurred towards the end of U.S. issue #3 and the beginning of U.S. issue #4, it was far better tied to the U.S. comic, picking up on how a couple characters seemed dissatisfied with their factions and spinning this dissatisfaction into a story. It continued directly into "Raiders of the Last Ark," also written by Furman. This story established one of the oddities of the original U.K. material, which was that very similar events would occur twice, in slightly different forms, with the U.K. version preceding the U.S. one. Thus, the Decepticons raided the Autobots' craft, the Ark, in "Raiders of the Last Ark," but retreated at the end — only to return in U.S. issue #4, where they were victorious over the Autobots.

Typically, new British stories ran 11 pages per issue, often continuing over many issues. To help stretch this first batch of original material, the story intended to run in U.K. issue #16 (the conclusion to "The Enemy Within!") was split over two issues, and this situation persisted through the rest of this batch of new material. ("Raiders of the Last Ark" was scripted as two 11-page chapters, but was run as four chapters of 5 or 6 pages.) For many years thereafter, 11 pages remained the standard in the U.K. title — which proved popular enough that it soon shifted to weekly publication and to full color. After this initial batch of new stories, most U.K. stories clearly took place between U.S. stories and were printed between those U.S. reprints, so that the confusion of *when* these earliest U.K. stories took place would generally be avoided.

Eventually, the U.K. series would change format several more times. But for most of its run, it was a weekly color title that published all-new 11-page stories between reprints of U.S. issues, which were each split into two segments. Because the monthly U.S. title was reprinted over two weeks, this meant that the British series (augmented by annuals) produced roughly as much new material as the American series for several years. Since the U.S. series ignored the U.K. one, continuity problems kept resulting, which the U.K. series attempted to solve or to avoid in different ways as it continued. Eventually, Simon Furman, the U.K. title's main writer, took over the U.S. series, writing it through its conclusion (#80, July 1991).

Throughout the U.S. title's run, American readers (such as myself) had no access to the original U.K. material. In the late 1990s, Transformers fans (some of the most hardcore fans around) scanned the U.K. (and U.S.) material, making it available online. Later, after Transformers comics experienced a wildly successful revival at Dreamwave, the original U.S. material would get trade paperback collections, after which much of the original U.K. material would was collected too. Once the Transformers comics license moved to IDW, it reprinted the original U.K. material over several mini-series and collected editions. But back in the 1980s, the only way most American comics readers knew the U.K. comic even *existed* was that it was listed in mail-order back-issue catalogs.

The great exception to this was "Man of Iron." In 1987, the U.S. series was doing very well, both creatively and commercially. Many of the most fondly remembered issues of that title were published in 1987. *Transformers: The Movie* had been released the year before — and gotten its own three-issue adaptation from Marvel. Marvel also released the mini-series *G.I. Joe and the Transformers* at the end of 1986. Marvel also published *Transformers Universe*, a four-issue mini-series featuring profile pages. And in 1987, the new Headmasters line of toys debuted in their own four-issue, bimonthly mini-series, *Transformers: Headmasters*, which was written by Bob Budiansky, writer of the main U.S. title. But the workload proved too much for him, and the U.S. title needed a fill-in issue or two at short notice.

As a result, issue #32 (Sept 1987) ended with a "next issue" blurb advertising the continuation of the then-running storyline. But instead of this appearing next, issues #33-34 (Oct-Nov 1987) reprinted "Man of Iron." What was originally going to run in issue #33 ran instead in issue #35 (Dec 1987). The two-month break was enough to get Budiansky back on track.

Running a British story as a U.S. fill-in was an inspired idea. It was cheaper and faster than commissioning a couple new fill-in issues. But it also gave U.S. readers a glimpse of this British material. In the Marvel tradition, issue #33 played this up, spinning what might rightly have been an embarrassment as if Marvel was doing its readers a favor. The cover to issue #33 even placed a Union Jack behind Grimlock in the corner of the cover.

You might wonder why the U.S. series didn't reprint a more recent U.K. story. After all, they were just as available and were designed to slip between U.S. stories. But the U.K. series had developed its own continuity, largely consistent with U.S. continuity but to its side. U.K. stories weren't side stories of little long-term consequence; they had their own continuing plots, which could have been wildly confusing to those who had only read the U.S. material. So why not go back to the beginning, before this continuity accumulated?

Some Transformers fans have mocked the two-issue reprint. And it's true that the two covers bore *no* resemblance to what was inside. Also, "Man of Iron" was originally printed mostly in black-and-white (with a few colored pages), but it had since been colored for British reprints. Instead of using these nicely colored pages, Marvel recolored the issue, which seems to have been done hastily and contained several errors. Also, the U.S. comic was printed on cheap paper, using Ben-Day dots, whereas the U.K. series used better printing methods. As a result, there's no comparing the quality of the two-issue reprint to its British equivalents.

But Americans hadn't seen this material. And as a ten-year-old boy, it *blew my mind*.

Sure, I was annoyed that the ongoing storyline (which was really good) was delayed. And it was certainly odd, to say the least, to have two entire issues, published three years into a title, that took place during the very first issues.

But once I got into the story, I realized very quickly that it was the most sophisticated Transformers story I'd ever read.

"Man of Iron" was written by Steve Parkhouse, who's mostly known for his work in British comics, including *2000AD* and on Doctor Who comics. He also illustrated *The Bojeffries Saga*, which was written by Alan Moore, and worked on the Night Raven character with David Lloyd. "Man of Iron" might have been written in the early days of Transformers comics, but its literary bent was immediately apparent.

The first page of "Man of Iron." Art by John Ridgway.

Right from the story's start, it's infused with a sense of history. The very first panel asks us to imagine this way in which the castle depicted is located at a specific place within a long timeline: "Who knows how many feet had trodden these paths in its nine hundred year history... or how many had been broken on its bleak stone walls?" This sense of being surrounded by history is something unknown to Americans, although it's common in Europe. And for the Americans gobbling up this story as a representative of British Transformers comics, this sense helped identify the story as uniquely European. Right off the start, this isn't a story that could have happened in America.

What American readers didn't know was that this was totally exceptional, in terms of British Transformers comics — most of which took place in America, since that's where the Transformers usually operated. Even in most European fantasy and science fiction, Europe is often little more than a backdrop. The castle, seen at the beginning of "Man of Iron," could easily have been simply a spooky setting in which to have a Decepticon skulking around. Instead, what's relevant about the castle is its historical depth, and the story wisely begins by setting the tone and creating an ambiance that gives an added depth to all that follows.

And this is key to the story, in which a Transformer has been lurking beneath the hills, not unlike a slumbering King Arthur.

While I've praised Steve Parkhouse, I haven't yet mentioned the story's artists. The first two 11-page chapters of "Man of Iron" were illustrated by the brilliant John Ridgway. Ridgeway has worked on many titles over the years, including *2000AD* (where he illustrated some of the most important Judge Dredd stories). He's perhaps best known to American readers as the inaugural artist on *Hellblazer*. His work is incredibly realistic, and it has a classical style, especially in terms of his shading, that worked perfectly with Parkhouse's more literary script.

The final two chapters were illustrated by Mike Collins, who's also done extensive work for British comics but who's had a career in the states as well (including *Uncanny X-Men* #266, featuring the first appearance of Gambit). Collins's style isn't quite as well-suited to "Man of Iron" as Ridgway, but he did a good job adapting to the material, and he produced some truly stunning panels.

In the story's first chapter, the three (original) Decepticon jets fly by Stansham Castle, which has been reduced to a small-town tourist attraction. One of the bombs buries itself into the ground. In a series in which planes and tanks explode all the time, this is hardly especially dramatic stuff. Yet Parkhouse and Ridgway do a fantastic job of selling the events. After building up how quiet the castle is these days, we watch the castle's guard react in alarm as the bombs are dropped, and we feel his alarm. We then watch the small town respond, as if seeing wheels set into motion that usually sit still.

The second half of the first chapter focuses on Sammy Harker, the young son of the castle's curator. He's playing with bows and arrows in the local forest. Pursuing an arrow up a tree, he finds himself face-to-face with Jazz. Illustrated by Ridgway, Jazz had never looked more like a real, three-dimensional, giant being. And it wasn't hard to imagine how frightening seeing his face staring at you might be, especially when high in a tree, where one would least expect such an encounter.

Young Sammy Harker comes face-to-face with Jazz, in what's essentially a jump scare. Art by John Ridgway.

In response, Sammy drops to the ground and flees. Jazz says nothing throughout the sequence, but we see him stepping on Sammy's discarded bow, cementing his menacing nature. Accenting this, Sammy finds Jazz following him out of the forest. Sammy runs, and Ridgway's art brilliantly conveys a child's breathless fear. He runs all the way home. Then, menacingly, we see Jazz pull up in car mode — and in the chapter's final panel, see that it has no driver.

It's hard to imagine a toy manufacturer okaying this depiction of one of its good guys scaring and stalking a little boy. It's totally out of sync with how the Autobots are generally portrayed. And that's why it works so remarkably well. The Autobots are, like all Transformers, giant alien robots. They're potentially frightening, especially to a young boy. But they're also alien, unfamiliar how frightening they may seem – or how to reassure young boys.

As the second chapter begins, Sammy wakes from a dream and walks onto his roof, where he sees an extraterrestrial craft pass overhead. It's a creepy sequence, and it has far more in common with stories of UFOs than it has with most Transformers stories.

Sammy sees the Transformers as a UFO in a surreal sequence.

Sammy then sees a Decepticon jet parked in his yard, and we wonder if it's been there throughout this sequence, or why Sammy hasn't noticed it before. In the next panel, we then see Sammy sleeping in his bed, although it's is now outside.

The Autobot Mirage then walks through the town, towering over its buildings. He's first seen in silhouette, which makes him seem more threatening. Like Jazz in the end of the first chapter, Mirage doesn't speak. He lumbers through the town. As he does, a panel shows Sammy talking in his sleep, apparently telling Mirage to get away. This would seem to suggest that Sammy's dreaming all of this, but why would he be dreaming himself asleep in his dream?

We then see Mirage outside Sammy's house. It's a legitimately frightening moment, in which we realize this alien is coming for Sammy. Next, we see Mirage peering into Sammy's window. This echoes Sammy's earlier face-to-face meeting with Jazz. Mirage says, "Sammy..." – and it's hard not to read this as a whisper, or like the sound of the wind. It's actually the first time a Transformer has spoken in the story. Ambiance is everything here, and the story (thanks in large part to Ridgway's art) pulls this off as very few comics do.

Sammy wakes up and shouts, but his bed begins to float. It's like a scarier version of *Little Nemo in Slumberland*. As Sammy grips his blanket, he seems to be pulled out through the open window, as if there's a gravity pulling him towards the Transformers, and he can't escape. His room is in chaos, with objects flying around — including a piece of paper with a crudely drawn robot on it, holding a torch and breathing fire, while battling knights at the local castle. The drawing floats through the window, and it's gripped by a robotic hand — a disembodied one, due to the panel border.

Sammy's parents, responding to the commotion, find their son's door locked. Forcing it open, they find Sammy in bed, although it's in disarray. The window's open and paper is flying around. Sammy's father goes to close the window... and his face freezes in shock. Outside, Mirage exits the house's yard, then walks off.

In his capacity as the castle's curator, Sammy's father arrives at the castle and finds the military busy there. Scanning the hill in search of the "unexploded bomb" dropped by the jet, the military's found "a very large object." Asked how large, we're told it's about the size of an ocean liner. There's a palpable sense of life having come unglued in this small town, and yet the story's only approached the Transformers tangentially.

At the end of the second chapter, Sammy sees Jazz, in car mode, on the street. Sammy's thought balloons recognize the car as a Porsche — a sign of the power of branding, but also a convincing reason for a young boy, interested in cars, to be enticed. He notices that the car has no rear-view mirror, nor side mirrors (or "driving mirror" and "wing mirrors," as Sammy's thoughts put it). This is presumably because the Autobots drive themselves and don't require mirrors to see behind them, but Parkhouse doesn't seem to know (at this early stage of Transformers history) that the entire point of the Autobots assuming the form of human cars was to *hide*. It's not their natural forms, and leaving off mirrors defeats the purpose. Still, it's a clever idea, suggesting that something's *wrong* – not just different but *wrong* – with this car.

Looking inside the car, Sammy sees that there's no speedometer. What's actually depicted is a completely alien control panel, in lieu of a dash. Again, this might go against the entire idea of "robots in disguise," but it's a cool idea that the Transformers' vehicle forms would seem somehow off, somehow alien. (Of course, the steering wheel is on the car's right, in the British fashion, which goes against the traditional depiction of the Transformers. It's not impossible that Jazz's vehicle form were redesigned for the Autobots' visit to England, although depictions of the Transformers have often ignored how easy it would probably be for the Transformers to make such modifications.)

Adding to the sequence's eerie feeling, Sammy finds his drawing of a fire-breathing robot in the car's back seat. Presumably, Mirage has given it to Jazz, but its presence connects Jazz to Sammy's spooky dream.

Next, the car door swings open by itself, and the car says, "Get in, Sammy!" It calls him by name. Jazz reassures Sammy that "There's nothing to be afraid of." But the Autobots' creepiness doesn't end here. Jazz sounds like a creepy man when he tries to convince Sammy to get inside: "Why not? It's a nice day... and you're on holiday." Sammy explains his mother told him "not to take lifts from strangers." Continuing his impression of a creepy man, Jazz asserts that he's not a stranger. "Why not just sit for a while in the front seat?" Jazz asks. "Just *pretend* you're driving..." Sammy gets in, and he enjoys pretending he's driving a Porsche. Jazz asks a question about the "men at the castle," and Sammy answers.

Then Sammy's mother comes out, alarmed. Jazz slams his own door, trapping Sammy inside. It's a mother's nightmare, and Sammy's mother shouts for her son to get out. He stares in alarm through the window at her, apparently unable to comply because

Jazz has locked his doors — or perhaps lacks door handles on the inside, like the way he lacks mirrors! And then Jazz drives off with Sammy inside.

It's perhaps the ultimate illustration of how the story's willing to depict the Autobots as alien and as threatening. But here, even the U.K. editors seem to have noticed that there may have been a problem, and a warning was added under the chapter's final page, which was reprinted along with the rest of the story for its U.S. edition: "Remember: never accept lifts from strangers!" The effect, however, underlines that the Autobots think little of *child abduction*.

The end of the second chapter of "Man of Iron." Art by John Ridgway.

But for anyone who complains that the Autobots aren't depicted as friendly enough, it's important to remember that "friendliness" is something measured in human terms. These Autobots have only recently arrived on Earth, and there's a lot they still don't understand. They're aliens, and their sense of propriety isn't going to be the same — especially given the exigencies of the situation — as our own.

This isn't a story about Autobots battling Decepticons. It's about how they and their conflict affect this small town, and these characters, in unexpected ways. And the feeling this creates for the reader is closer to that of *Close Encounters of the Third Kind* than the usual melodramatic robot battles. Indeed, there's something distinctly Spielbergian about the story, right down to its focus on the human element and its willingness to tie the good guys to a child's fear. And how cool is it to find a prolonged – and effective – dream sequence in a Transformers story?

Compared to U.S. stories, "Man of Iron" is willing to be what would later be called "decompressed." At this point, we're 22 pages – a full U.S. issue – into the story. Ostensibly, very little has happened. A couple bombs have been dropped, but mostly what they've done is scare people and lead them to discover that something large is buried there. Sammy's been the focus, and the Transformers have barely spoken, let alone fought.

As chapter three begins, Jazz continues to talk with Sammy, whom the Autobot is effectively holding prisoner. Jazz explains that he was the robot he saw in the woods. In a little but nice gesture towards the Transformers' alien origins, Jazz explains that his real name "is unpronounceable in your language." Mirage and Trailbreaker, also in their car forms, join Jazz.

Next, we get the story's first Autobot-Decepticon fight. The Decepticon jets spot the Autobots and attack. One blasts Trailbreaker, and it looks like a particularly savage hit. Trailbreaker transforms, and in a brutally effective image, we see him smoking, his face shielded in shadow. It's a far more realistic depiction of Transformers violence than what's since become conventional. Of course, this also underlines the threat to Sammy, who wouldn't have survived such a hit, thus helping to raise the sequence's stakes.

Mirage disappears (a trait seen on the TV show but not generally shown in the comic), and this spurs one Decepticon jet to crash into a bridge.

Another jet blasts at Jazz, but Sammy jerks the wheel, helping Jazz to dodge. It's a bit absurd that Sammy, who's never driven a car before, would be able to dodge better than Jazz, and we're inclined to think that Sammy simply gets lucky. Still, at least it gives him something to do, and it helps to sell the fantasy of encountering the Transformers, after the fear of the story's first half.

Bluestreak then drives across an overpass, transforms, and uses a gun to take down the final Decepticon jet. The jet crashes to the ground, landing in a fiery wreck. Again, the story's far more realistic and more brutal than what we've since become accustomed. While these vehicles are treated as alien Transformers, they're also depicted as similarly fragile to Earth vehicles. They don't shrug off blasts. Their metal tears apart, and they burn.

Finally, Jazz arrives at the Autobot camp — by which point, Sammy has fallen asleep. An Autobot craft is waiting, and it's a curved vehicle like the one Sammy dreamed about — something at home in UFO stories but not in Transformers ones. Jazz explains the ship is only a "shuttlecraft." A hatch opens, swinging outward along the curved surface of the craft, again like a UFO. And Optimus Prime emerges.

That's how we first see Optimus Prime — like an alien, emerging from a UFO.

Sammy's brought inside the craft, and we see him sitting on one of its giant seats. There's a sense of realism here, of hard science fiction, which tends to think of little implications such as the size of alien seats. Okay, the seat isn't really big *enough* — but the idea is there.

Jazz asks Sammy about the drawing, and the boy responds that it's "been around the castle since historic times." Sammy adds, "He's sort of a *legend*." The similarity between the large robot in the drawing looks like the Autobots, and Optimus Prime explains that, after arriving on Earth, they picked up a signal in their language from this small town. Optimus speculates that it was a *"rescue craft"* sent in search of the rest of them. Obviously, it's what's hidden beneath the hills that the military has discovered. When Sammy points this out, Optimus Prime is obviously concerned; he warns that, if the humans unearth the craft, the Decepticons will destroy it and the entire village around it.

It's not clear why the Decepticons wouldn't be able to track the craft as easily as the Autobots, or why they'd wait to unleash their fury until the humans discovered the ship. But it's a cool idea that Cybertron would send a ship after its missing leadership. It's part of the original Transformers story that the Ark was buried and largely inactive on Earth for millions of years, so there was plenty of time for another ship to arrive. This would seem to be an obvious idea, yet it's one that's rarely been used in Transformers lore.

As the final chapter of "Man of Iron" begins, the British military has unearthed a portion of the side of the buried spacecraft. It's now clear that the hill in question formed *over* the craft; its shape has defined the hill, the contours of the land. That's how long it's been there. And on the ship's exposed hull, we see an ancient and tattered Autobot symbol.

In another indicator of how early this story is set, the military thinks the craft may be extraterrestrial, with no reference to the presence of the Transformers — as if that's not yet public knowledge.

Then there's a rumbling, as if from an earthquake, and a square portion of the ground lifts up, on the top of the craft... exposing the Man of Iron, the Autobot that Sammy drew. Using a pistol, it attacks a military vehicle — perhaps uncharacteristic for an Autobot, but another sign of how alien he is from Earth culture. It may also reflect past conflicts with humans, if Sammy's drawings reflect an actual violent encounter during the Medieval period.

One of the Decepticon jets arrives, in robot form, and blasts the Man of Iron. Here again, the violence of this story — and the damage it does to the Transformers — remains realistic and heightened, relative to later Transformers stories. The Decepticon's blast severs the Man of Iron's right leg at the knee.

The Decepticon fires again, blasting the Man of Iron down. Another blast tears the Man of Iron apart.

It's a shocking — and upsetting — development. This is the first time we've actually seen the Man of Iron, and the Decepticon appears and kills the Autobot on a single page. This may also be seen as reflecting the brutal realism of the story's violence; in real-world armed conflicts, death can come quickly and without giving the wounded any opportunity for last-minute speeches or heroics. But this sudden death is also sad, because we've been made to understand that the Man of Iron has been there at least for centuries. He's an undiscovered mystery of human history, and he's killed without a second thought. It's a little like if the Loch Ness Monster were discovered – and then gunned down.

The fact that the Decepticon (like so many Transformers in this story) doesn't speak only cements the evil of the deed. This is the Decepticon's mission, and he doesn't need to talk or to gloat. He's just there to kill.

The story then cuts to the Autobots' shuttlecraft, flying low to the ground along a road. It lowers a ramp, allowing Jazz to roll out onto the street in his car form. Sammy's inside, but he jumps clear before Jazz rolls over a hill and slams into the Decepticon who killed the Man of Iron. Meanwhile, a group of Decepticons, including Laserbeak, dive bombs the Autobot shuttlecraft, but manned guns emerge from its hull, and it blasts the Decepticons (or at least Laserbeak). On the ground, Jazz has transformed, and he fires a rocket into the air, hitting one of the Decepticon jets, who's flying in his robot form.

We're then treated to a single large panel, depicting the battle from overhead and focused on the Autobot shuttlecraft. It's a pretty glorious panel, with various Decepticons blasting the shuttle, as Autobots blast back from its hull. And the battle occurs over the English countryside, successfully conveying a sense of rural community enmeshed in the Transformers' war. The captions underline this impression: "The castle of Stansham once again bore witness to the sight and sound of battle... / A flaming, wheeling dance of destruction." There's a sense of Biblical conflict here, and we see a Decepticon jet apparently crash into the castle, reminding us that this historic building has been placed in jeopardy.

And then the Decepticons flee.

It's amazing to think that the entire conflict, from when Jazz hits the Decepticon to when the Decepticons flee, takes up only two pages – out of a 44-page story. It would have been easy, especially given the decompressed nature of the story, to have taken an extra chapter to depict the fight, in order to give some sense of a wild climax. To some extent, this is part of the larger problem that this final chapter feels rushed, and not simply in this two-page sequence. But the speed of the battle also works *for* the story, which is about Sammy, ambiance, and alien encounters more than Autobot-Decepticon battle. There's an awful lot of conflict in this chapter, but all of it's rapid. Even in the wild, climactic battle, the specifics of the fight aren't as important as the juxtaposition between it and this rural community.

What we're reading is less about seeing specific Transformers fight it out and more about the impression of a wild extraterrestrial battle in the skies over this town — a battle this community can't understand and certainly can't influence.

In another sign that this is an early story, Optimus Prime uses the violence as an illustration of how they can't simply leave Earth to the Decepticons — as if this were even in question, or even as if this were the Autobots' plan until things escalated.

Optimus Prime adds that they cannot leave the rescue ship intact — presumably, to avoid it falling into Decepticon hands... but also possibly to avoid it falling into human hands.

With Optimus set to destroy the ship, we cut to a chamber inside it, where we see that another Autobot resides. Captions tell us that the Man of Iron was simply his attendant and that he was the ship's navigator. He seems to be in a sort of slumber, or suspended animation, and we're told that, "In his long, slow, machine world, a million years were as fleeting seconds. Human history had passed over him." It's an indication of temporal relativity, to accent the story's focus on cultural relativity, on the alien nature of the Transformers.

The Navigator is described as being "alone in the darkness," and he's apparently the source of the signal the Autobots picked up — which he's still beaming out.

On the top of the final page, we're shown Jazz pointing his rocket launcher downward at the rescue ship. Painfully, the first caption tells us: "Jazz could know nothing of us. He only knew of his friendship with a small boy… / …and what could happen if his enemies prevailed." He fires, obliterating the ship – and the Autobot slumbering within it.

The next panel shows Jazz in the same position before he fired, only now the rocket is gone from the smoking launcher, and where the craft was is smoking too. The caption is succinct: "Nothing remained."

It's true that the Navigator's death is unnecessary. Presumably, the Autobots cannot read that he's aboard, perhaps because of the Navigator's suspended animation. But it's surprising that they aren't aware such systems exist, and that they didn't bother to search the craft. Still, we wouldn't have this complaint if the Navigator weren't introduced, on the penultimate page. He's there to die.

But in a story that dares to alienate us from the Autobots, this is the final alienation. The Autobots unknowingly kill one of their own. It's a sad ending, but it's also a sophisticated move to let *us* know something that the Autobots don't.

The Navigator goes unmourned. He's yet another victim of a conflict, in which even the good-guy Autobots are warriors following orders.

And war's not a pretty thing. The Navigator's death completely undercuts any sense of heroic victory, which is common not only to Transformers stories but to plenty of stories of super-powered conflict.

It's possible that the Navigator's death was intended to represent a lost opportunity for the Transformers to return home. This is supported by Optimus Prime's comments about fleeing Earth, and by how he explains to Sammy that the Transformers "are *stranded* here on Earth." That's technically true, in the early Transformers stories: the Ark, the ship that brought the Transformers to Earth, is no longer capable of flight. But these stories aren't preoccupied with the Transformers' desire to return home. In this respect, "Man of Iron" might suggest a misunderstanding of the Transformers formula, or an alternate take on it. On the other hand, as an early Transformers story, these overtones suggest the freshness of the Autobots' arrival and hint that they *miss* Cybertron, for which they seem nostalgic. The Navigator's death might thus be taken as representative of the loss of the Transformers' home.

But there's a deeper way of interpreting the Navigator's death. His ship was a *rescue ship*. And the Autobots destroy it. In doing so, they're denying their own rescue. They're committing to staying on Earth and continuing the war with the Decepticons there. There's no escape from this war, and this story — certainly more than any other early Transformers story — illustrates how terrible this war can be and how quickly it can claim lives, including those of the Transformers.

The rest of the final page is a masterpiece of an ending. The story, which has enmeshed the Transformers into a historical context, telescopes itself into the future. And the story denies itself any of the platitudes, jokes, and easy constructions of meaning so common to pop-culture endings:

> Instructions were issued by nameless authorities... trucks came... all traces of the craft and its final resting place were obliterated...
> Summer came around again... the tourists descended, attracted by stories of *U.F.O.s* and mysterious sightings...
> The found only an empty ruin, echoing with memories.
> Autumn came... leaves fell... Sammy was a year older and a year wiser. He never saw Jazz again...
> But on clear, sharp nights, when stars glittered like needles and the night winds rattled his window...
> Then he slept a fitful, fearful sleep...
> ...And the Man of Iron walked once more through his dreams.

Of course, Sammy's been the emotional center of the story from the beginning, so it's fitting that the story should end with him, instead of the conventional focus on the more esoteric Transformers. The fact that "he never saw Jazz again" reflects the fate of so many children, who have been featured in Transformers stories, only to never appear again.

In the language of "stars glitter[ing] like needles," we can see the sense of wonder that's so much a part of science-fiction stories, including those of the Transformers. And in "the night winds rattl[ing] his window," we can see the sense of fear and horror, the flipside of wonder that also accompanies the new. These are both a part of the "dreams," the word on which the story ends, which is both a dream, in the positive sense, and a nightmare.

There's a real sense that Sammy's haunted here, cemented by the image of the dead Man of Iron over the sleeping Sammy in the final panel. Death pervades the ending, and not only in the death of the Navigator. Death is also there in the dead leaves of autumn. It's there in "empty ruin" left by the rescue craft, which the tourists come to see.

But isn't the appeal of historic sites, like Stansham Castle, an attraction to dead things? The story begins with this sense of history, and it ends with it too. Eventually, even the arrival of the alien Transformers must pass also into history, must be fitted into it — and perhaps alter it.

This is the perspective that "Man of Iron" provides.[*]

---

[*] First serialized on Sequart Organization's website in June 2014.

When "Tales of Cybertron" Explored the Transformers' Backstory

The original Transformers comic in the U.K. was augmented by hardcover annuals, beginning with *Transformers Annual 1986* (published in late 1985). These annuals generally included several short stories, some in the comics format and others in illustrated text, along with profile pages and sometimes a few game-like features, such as puzzles or pages readers could color.

For the first couple annuals, the Transformers was still new, and its continuity was very much in flux. The weekly U.K. series had enough difficulty interacting with the U.S. series, but the annuals had even more trouble. The U.S.-driven continuity essentially told a single story through 1985, leaving little room for new stories to be inserted between. Compounding this, Marvel U.K. almost certainly wanted to include new and popular characters, such as the Insecticons, which hadn't yet debuted in the U.S. The result, inevitably, were stories that featured a set of Transformers who couldn't be together, as well as inconsistencies. Making sure that the U.S. stories eventually connected with these U.K. stories was beneath the attention of the U.S. Marvel offices. But in fairness, the U.K. offices hardly seemed concerned either, and some stories in these annuals even conflicted with one another (as we'll soon see).

One of the stand-out stories from the very first annual was "And There Shall Come... a Leader!" The 10-page story was written by Simon Furman, who had already become the dominant U.K. Transformers writer — a position he'd hold throughout the U.K. series; in fact, he'd also take over the U.S. series. The short story was illustrated by John Stokes, and the characters have the feel of early Transformers art, in which the depictions are slightly closer to the actual toys than most of us are used to. Also, the story's splash page includes a robot in the background that's swiped from page 3 of *Transformers* #1.

That's actually kind of cool, however, because the short story was a prequel to *Transformers* #1, and the swiped art helps connect the two stories. The short story (like the earliest pages of *Transformers* #1) was set on Cybertron, prior to the events that led the Transformers to Earth. Specifically, the story focused on how Optimus Prime became Autobot leader. On the top of the story's second page, "Tales of Cybertron" was emblazoned upon the top of the page, indicating that this was something special.

Today, we're not surprised by the idea of a story set on Cybertron in the past. But at the time of the story's publication, this was something unique. True, a few animated episodes featured time travel to Cybertron's past, or glimpses thereof. But those were framed by their present-day sequences and case. The idea of an entire prequel story was popularized by the mini-series *Transformers: The War Within* (#1-6, Oct 2002 - Mar 2003), which wasn't published until Dreamwave's revival of Transformers comics. This original "Tale of Cybertron" appeared when the Transformers were still new.

In the story, the Decepticons, led by Megatron, are overrunning Cybertron, and its capitol city, Iacon, is in danger of falling. Bluestreak, in his Cybertronian form (which is a little too close to his human car form, but at least bothers to be somewhat different from it), is on a mission to deliver bombs to Optimus Prime, who was then an Autobot general. In a bit of violence rare to Transformers stories at the time, Bluestreak's comrade, Fusion, is killed during the mission. The Council of Autobot Elders decides to invest its whole authority in Optimus Prime. As Megatron prepares his final assault, Optimus Prime leads a counter-attack. Megatron blasts Optimus Prime, who orders that his Autobots flee. They do, but as Megatron's about to deliver the final blow, those previously-mentioned bombs detonate, collapsing the elevated road on which everyone was fighting. Apparently, Optimus Prime intended to sacrifice himself, and his order that the Autobots flee was to get them out of the way from the coming destruction. Naturally, we see that both Optimus Prime and Megatron have survived the destruction, and the final panel is of Optimus Prime, who's now Autobot leader.

TALES OF CYBERTRON

THE PLANET **CYBERTRON**, MILLIONS OF YEARS BEFORE THE **TRANSFORMERS** AWOKE TO THEIR EXILE ON EARTH...

THE **DECEPTICON** WAR MACHINE IS IN FULL ACTION; ONE BY ONE, THE GREAT CITY STATES OF THE **AUTOBOTS** ARE BEING OVERRUN – AND THE **DECEPTICONS** TAKE NO PRISONERS!

NOW, THE DECEPTICON FORCES HAVE LAUNCHED WHAT COULD BE THEIR FINAL OFFENSIVE, AGAINST THE CAPITAL CITY ITSELF... **IACON**.

WE ARE DOOMED...

AND WITHIN THE HEAVILY PROTECTED CELESTIAL TEMPLE, THE COUNCIL OF AUTOBOT ELDERS IS IN SESSION... FOR WHAT MAY BE THE LAST TIME!

THE DECEPTICONS HAVE BREACHED ALL BUT OUR FINAL DEFENCES. OUR TROOPS ARE IN DISARRAY – WE ARE DEFEATED!

NEVER!

EMIRATE XAARON...

OUR FORCES ARE IN DISARRAY BECAUSE FOOLS LIKE YOU, TOMAANDI, INSIST ON COUNCIL CONTROL...

WE MUST LET THEM OFF OUR LEASH... ENTRUST CONTROL TO AN INDIVIDUAL... A **WARRIOR!**

From "And There Shall Come... a Leader!" Art by John Stokes.

JULIAN DARIUS | 33

That final caption tells us, "never once did Optimus Prime shirk the responsibility that had been handed to him," and the story obviously intends us to view him as heroic, especially since he's willing to sacrifice himself. We're supposed to enjoy this story about how Optimus Prime became leader of the Autobots and not think too much about it. But the story actually presents a far more complex portrait of this moment.

Today, we're probably used to thinking about the Autobots as *always* having a singular leader. That's how the cartoon presented things, placing Optimus Prime and then Rodimus Prime as part of a long continuity of such leaders. Many stories have since suggested that "Prime" is an indicator of this leadership role, or at least the potential to assume it. In essence, this presents the Autobots' system of government as a monarchy. And although Transformers don't have children, Autobot monarchs alone determine their successors. For example, when Optimus Prime appoints Ultra Magnus his successor in *Transformers: The Movie*, nobody questions this, even after Ultra Magnus's rule deteriorates.

"And There Shall Come... a Leader!" suggests something quite different. There, we're led to believe that the Council of Autobot Elders ruled the Autobots before ceding sole authority to Optimus Prime. Optimus was already a prominent general, apparently in charge of the capital city of Iacon. This transition parallels that between the Roman republic and the Roman empire. In other words, Optimus Prime is Julius Caesar.

This makes what we witness in the story far more morally ambiguous. Images of Rome tend to focus on its imperial period, but the transition from republic to empire is still debated today and is usually depicted as, at best, a necessary evil. Historically, Caesar's seizure of power was represented by his supporters as a temporary measure done in the name of the republic. Long after it was clear that Rome was permanently ruled by a monarch, some Romans continued to pine for the republic.

Optimus Prime may seem nobler and less power-hungry than how Julius Caesar is often depicted. The Council of Autobot Elders seems only too eager to cede its authority to its most prominent general, and there's no sign in the story that Optimus Prime has manipulated the council into this decision. Still, we shouldn't ignore that what we're witnessing, in the story, is the fall of the Autobot republic and the beginning of a dictatorship — even if it's usually depicted as a benevolent dictatorship.

While there's no sign that Optimus Prime is pulling the strings behind the Council's decision to divest its own authority, there are ominous signs that he may not be innocent. When Emirate Xaaron calls Optimus with the news that Optimus now has full control over the Autobot forces, Optimus replies "At last..." He's clearly waiting for the news. It's not unexpected. Indeed, Xaaron seems to be Optimus's inside man on the Council. True, Optimus's first response to the news is couched in the language of being released to help the Autobots: "At last, I can strike positively against the advancing Decepticons..." He's not self-congratulatory, nor hungry for power — at least not for its own sake. But there are clear indications that he wants the Council to make this decision and has been planning (plotting?) with Xaaron.

Then there's the Autobot, who looks a lot like Gears, who plants the actual bombs in the story. His thought balloons indicate that he and others have spent "weeks" securing the bombs and planning for this moment. "And all without the Council suspecting we were acting without their approval," he thinks. In other words, Optimus Prime's been defying the Council — and the law. Perhaps this was a necessary evil, but it certainly demonstrates that Optimus hasn't been respecting the existing government, while he's also been consulting on the Council's decision to cede all control to him personally.

What emerges from an examination of these undertones is something far different from what the story seems to wish to convey. We're supposed to see Optimus Prime as an uncomplicated hero and to see his becoming Autobot leader as a good thing. But reading between the lines, a very different picture emerges.

It's worth mentioning that there's no sign that the Decepticons, who generally transform into military vehicles, have ever been anything except a dictatorship. That makes sense. This story suggests that the more domestic Autobots' natural form of government is a republic. That republic's dissolution, the story suggests, was a necessity of war. And even if Optimus Prime is the most noble Transformer ever, we ought not to pretend that the Autobots haven't compromised their principles here. Essentially, almost everything we've seen of the Autobots is a new and recent state, necessitated by desperation.

At the very least, this suggests that mining the Transformers' time on Cybertron, prior to the series's beginning, could result in fascinating material — stories that had the capability of changing how we saw the Transformers. One of the problems with the Transformers, despite their obvious coolness and potential, has long been that their backstory was never worked out. "Tales of Cybertron" had the potential to do that.

But there would be only one more such story, produced almost a year later, for *Transformers Annual 1987*. This story was a prose tale with illustrations — a format common to British comics annuals. But despite this difference of medium, the story was very much a companion to "And There Shall Come… a Leader!" Only instead of focusing on Optimus Prime, this new story focused on Megatron. It's also set even *earlier*, before the Autobot-Decepticon war, so that it could be regarded as a prequel to "And There Shall Come… a Leader!" (which was itself a prequel to the rest of the series).

The story, entitled "State Games," ran 8 pages, was written by James Hill, and was illustrated by John Stokes (who also illustrated "And There Shall Come… a Leader!"). Whereas that earlier story was labeled "Tales of Cybertron" (on the top of its second page) this one is labelled "A Tale from Cybertron" right above the title on the story's first page.

The story establishes that the various cities of Cybertron used to conduct gladiatorial games, a mixture of the Greek Olympics and Roman gladiatorial combat. Interestingly, the story also establishes that Cybertron suffers from population pressured, caused by the unabated creation of new Transformers. (Regretfully, how new Transformers are created has varied over the years; most versions suggest some sort of Transformers "soul" is required, but that kind of mysticism is nicely absent from this story.)

In the story, Megatron is the champion athlete from the city of

Tarn, while Optimus Prime is the champion from Iacon. The Vos athletic team plots to plant a bomb in Tarn, where the games are being held. Although the Vos team intends to plant evidence suggesting Iacon was responsible for the bombing, they fail; the bomb goes off, decimating Tarn, but Vos's guilt becomes known. As a consequence, the cities of Tarn and Vos go to war, whereas the Tarn plot was intended to lead to a war between Tarn and Iacon. At the end of the story, the war between Tarn and Vos concludes, and Megatron convinces the survivors to form a new faction known as the Decepticons.

And thus the Autobot-Decepticon war begins.

The depiction of Cybertron's government here is at odds with what we've seen in "And There Shall Come... a Leader!" Before the creation of the Decepticons, we're shown that the Autobots are ruled by someone known only as the Autobot Overlord — although he's depicted as old and frail, requiring frequent care. The Overlord used to rule the entire planet, prior to the rise of city-states. By the time the story takes place, his power is largely ceremonial. The Overlord is left to die during the story, which doesn't explain how this is compatible with the Council seen in "And There Shall Come... a Leader!"

I love the idea that the various Cybertronian cities have their own culture, although that's barely explored in this story. As you can probably tell, I'm a sucker for examinations of Transformer history, society, and government. As robotic life, the Transformers are very alien, and the idea that aliens ought to be presented as having alien cultures with moralities foreign to our own is a foundational idea in science fiction. At eight pages, "State Games" is more suggestive of possibilities than fulfilling of them, but it's another example of how the Transformers could be made fascinating from a science-fiction standpoint.

Even though this was only a prose story in the second U.K. annual, it's one of the more influential Transformers stories. Beginning with Dreamwave's comics continuity, the idea that Decepticons evolved out of gladiatorial games has been a part of almost every version of the Transformers. IDW's 2007 four-issue mini-series *The Transformers: Megatron Origin* is essentially a reboot of "State Games," with the games — there illegal — and cultural turmoil serving as essential aspects of Megatron's rise to power.

Sadly, these were the only two "Tales of Cybertron" ever produced. But they're full of potential. The name "Tales of Cybertron" recalls "Tales of Asgard," the back-up that fleshed out Thor's backstory and first made Thor seem meaningfully different (or even alien) as a character. Had "Tales of Cybertron" continued, even as an annual concern, it could have had much the same effect. But even the two stories that were published infused the Transformers with new meaning, having lasting effects not only for the then-current comics continuity but for all the Transformers continuities that followed.*

---

* First published on Sequart Organization's website in June 2014.

On "The Night the Transformers Saved Christmas"

Surely among the least-known early Transformers comics, "The Night the Transformers Saved Christmas" appeared in the 26 December 1985 issue of *Woman's Day* magazine. The four-page story wasn't an insert; it was printed on page 69-72 of the magazine.

Why exactly a Transformers story, aimed at an audience predominantly composed of boys, would be printed in *Woman's Day* isn't entirely clear. But a banner across the first page's corner pronounced it a "kids' comic special," as if women reading the magazine might get to these four pages and hand the magazine over to their children.

The story was clearly prepared by Marvel Comics. It doesn't feature any credits, although some have identified the art as the product of artist Herb Trimpe, who did occasional work for the Marvel Transformers comic's early years. Among the oddities of the story is that, because it was printed in *Woman's Day*, which presumably used offset printing, the story's colors are superior to those of the ongoing Marvel comic, which was still printed on newsprint.

The story takes place on Christmas Eve, although no year is specified (which is convenient for continuity purposes, as we'll discuss below). The Perry family, who lives in an American town called Midville in an unspecified state, drives to their town square to witness the traditional lighting of the town Christmas tree. However, we see that the power's off in the town. (Readers would be forgiven for thinking that the Perry family had *arrived* in the town square and discovered the power out, but we later see that this isn't the case; the story simply jumps from the Perry family driving to the town square to show what they *haven't* yet seen. It's not the clearest of transitions.)

The reason for the power outage is soon made clear: the

Decepticons Soundwave and Laserbeak are siphoning the electricity from a nearby power station. In the very next panel, the Autobots Bumblebee, Tracks, and Hoist arrive. It's not entirely clear how the Autobots discovered the incident, nor why only these three Autobots would be sent. We're only told that Bumblebee "has been keeping his optical sensors" on Soundwave and summoned the others for help. Does this mean that Bumblebee's been stalking Soundwave and requested that only Tracks and Hoist come to assist him?

Soundwave's reaction to the Autobots' arrival is to immediately flee. He justifies this by telling Laserbeak that they're outnumbered.

In a nice touch, we're shown Soundwave transforming into his cassette tape mode, which Laserbeak takes in his mouth as he flies away. The reason this is a nice touch is that Laserbeak, whose alternate form is a cassette tape, is normally transported inside Soundwave. Reversing this takes advantage of the implicit size-changing inherent to most of the Transformers: when a cassette tape can unfold into a child-sized robot, it's obviously *growing* as well as changing shape. Many Transformers stories avoid drawing attention to this, since it's essentially a byproduct of the toy designs. In fact, many of the earliest Transformers toys were molds from existing Japanese toys lines that were simply combined into a new one, so there was no thought given to maintaining scale between the toys, let alone between the *two* forms of each toy.

As Laserbeak escapes, he fires a blast that downs a tree along the secluded road. It falls in front of the Perry's car, on its way to the town square's Christmas tree. The Perry family gets out of its car and is clearly scared of the giant yellow robot standing in the road. Bumblebee reassures them and takes the fallen tree off the hood of the Perry's car. But the car's no longer operational; or, as Bumblebee amusingly puts it, "I fear your car is unconscious."

(Strictly speaking, Bumblebee should probably know by now that human cars aren't, you know, *alive*. He already knows what humans are, after all. But Bumblebee's line evokes one of the best features of the earliest Transformers stories, in which Optimus Prime and the rest assume that Earth's vehicles are its dominant life form — a perfectly reasonable assumption on their part, and one that illustrates the truly alien perspective of the Transformers. Bumblebee's dialogue here, while amusing, therefore also evokes one of the best elements of the Transformers story. And it's only a single line, so it may pretty easily be forgiven as Bumblebee slipping momentarily into older thought patterns, in which a non-functional car might well be considered to be "unconscious.")

Cynthia Perry, the mother of the family, requests a ride into town. "We have to deliver these presents," she explains. When Bumblebee prompts her for more information, she adds that on Christmas Eve, "everyone goes to town and puts a present under the Christmas tree for those in need."

The story's dripping with the wholesome goodness associated with traditional Americana, and I must add that I've lived in many different parts of America, including small towns, and never seen anything like this. Most small towns don't have a central Christmas tree, and I'm unaware of any that put presents for the needy under it. But it's a *wonderful* idea, filled with the kind of neighborly compassion for the less fortunate that ought to be a part of Christmas.

Bumblebee's apparently equally impressed. "That's a very nice tradition," he says. "We have nothing like it back where I come from on Cybertron." But Bumblebee soon realizes the problem when Cynthia adds that "the best part is when the Christmas tree lights are turned on!"

On the final page, Prowl has joined Tracks and Hoist, who says that "those human engineers should be able to complete repairs on the power lines better than us, Prowl." It's a little odd, given that we don't see these "human engineers." Essentially, the Autobots have just left the problem for the humans to deal with. The same word balloon could just as easily tell us that the Autobots had repaired the power station between panels, but that would upset the plot. Rather than concern themselves with repairs, the Autobots are instead concerned with where Bumblebee has gone. Apparently, he's driven the Perry family into town without a single word to his comrades, who have to follow Bumblebee's tracks in the snow to find him.

They find Bumblebee in the town square, where he's hooked up the Christmas tree to his battery. Because Bumblebee's car form is a Volkswagen Beetle, his battery is in his trunk — a rare bit of fidelity to the particulars of the Transformers' vehicle forms. Lest we miss the point of the story, Bumblebee, asked what he's doing, says that "the humans would call it 'giving to those in need'!"

The final page of "The Night the Transformers Saved Christmas."

After Bumblebee charmingly refers to the tree as "that organic structure," he ends the strip by exclaiming, *"Merry Christmas, Autobots!"*

It's only a four-issue story, and it's certainly got its clunky moments. For example, the Perry family, which ought to be the human grounding of the story, disappears on this final page, where they could at least be shown smiling, if not handing out presents to the less fortunate or something.

And as a Transformers story, there's not much in the way of drama. The Decepticon plan is pretty pathetic. We've seen them take over offshore drilling rigs and the like, so siphoning electricity from a regional substation is small potatoes. Compounding this, there's no fight at all; the Decepticons simply run away as soon as the Autobots arrive. The only shot that's fired is the one Laserbeak uses to down the tree that disables the Perry family's car, presumably to get the Autobots to focus on the endangered (or at least inconvenienced) humans rather than on pursuing the Decepticons.

But it's this same concern for humans that helps redeem the story. Sure, it's all a whitewashed, slightly syrupy version of wholesome, small-town America. But the entire *reason* why such visions are wholesome is because of the good-hearted, unpretentious, communal concern for the less fortunate that we're told the town's Christmas tree ritual represents. Sure, the focus ends up being on the pretty lights of the town tree. But underneath this celebration, and grafted to it, is a very basic kind of humanitarianism.

Yes, it's an easy form of sacrifice. Bringing some presents, one day a year, isn't that much more difficult than Bumblebee letting humans strap some cables to his batteries. But it's something, and its heart is in the right place. It's amazing how this aspect of the town's Christmas tree, only present in Cynthia Perry's dialogue, redeems the story, or at least keeps it from collapsing.

Having been prepared by Marvel Comics, "The Night the Transformers Saved Christmas" actually fits relatively well into Marvel's comics continuity. It can't, however, occur in the year in which it was published, 1985. Tracks and Hoist didn't debut until

1986. The story *must* occur in 1986, because Bumblebee would become Goldbug in 1987.

Since it's not even known exactly *who* made "The Night the Transformers Saved Christmas," it's not surprising we also don't know precisely *when* it was made. *Woman's Day* probably required a bit more lead time than most Marvel comics in 1985 operated with. In any case, this is one of the earliest Transformers comics stories, and its fascinating for that reason.

The story doesn't have the awkwardness of the very earliest stories, in which artists conformed a bit too closely to the toys. Still, when Soundwave transforms, his transformation looks very much like his toy counterpart. Bumblebee's reference to the Perrys' car being "unconscious" and the tree as "that organic structure" also help this feel like an early story. The story's title alone makes it a classic.

The U.S. Marvel, unlike its U.K. division (which had its own Transformers comic), didn't publish short Transformers stories, helping to make this story even more of an oddity. Marvel U.K.'s Transformers comic would eventually print five Christmas stories, beginning the same year "The Night the Transformers Saved Christmas" was published and continuing until 1989. But this was the only Transformers Christmas story produced by the U.S. Marvel Comics – and it's one that almost no Transformers fan has read.[*]

---

[*] First published on Sequart Organization's website in December 2013.

When the Transformers Got Religion

There are a lot of reasons why *Transformers: The Movie* was revolutionary, when it was released in 1986.

Its level of animation was spectacular for anything but a Disney film. *Akira* hadn't yet been released, and there was simply nothing like *Transformers: The Movie* out there. Optimus Prime transformed and flipped through the air, the camera rotating around him, while he fired on Decepticon after Decepticon.

The movie was just as different audibly. It had brilliant synthesizer-heavy instrumentals, composed by Vince DiCola, as well as a rock soundtrack that ran the gamut from "Weird Al" Yankovic, through the fast-paced but upbeat Stan Bush, to several more hard-rock bands. The combination of such music and high-quality animation blew a lot of young minds.

Transformers: The Movie was also shockingly violent; the TV show avoided death, but characters were mowed down in the movie in huge numbers, and they fell with anguished expressions and smoking wounds. Famously, this included the death of Autobot leader Optimus Prime – traumatizing a generation of children, some of whom broke down in tears in the theaters. Behind the scenes, this was justified by making way for the characters based on new toys – but it's what's on screen that matters, and what's on screen was a movie a lot closer to the violence of *RoboCop* than the kid-friendly TV show.

The movie also *radically* altered the Transformers story. Transformers had always been a science-fiction story, but it had been set in the present and predominantly on Earth. Now, the narrative jumped forward almost 20 years to 2005, and featured more outer-space settings. Features like Cybertron's moons suddenly became important, and the story ended with the Autobots having reclaimed Cybertron. A brand new faction, the Quintessons, was introduced. And of course, the leaders of *both* factions were killed off and replaced.

Optimus Prime spontaneously turned grey upon dying, the life and color drained out of him. No other Transformer (even in the movie) did this upon dying, which *might* be explained by the removal of the Matrix but *certainly* had the effect of driving the knife deeper into kids' hearts.

The story also took on generational aspects. The story's main human character, a young man, was suddenly the father of a boy. Kup and Hot Rod represented an older and younger generation of Transformers, neither of which had previously been seen. Then there was the changing of the guard, as both factions changed leaders.

All of this blew my eight-year-old mind. And in many ways, still does.

But for me, probably the most radical aspect of the movie was that the Transformers had *their own religion*.

It would be easy — and not inaccurate — to say that the original conceit of the Transformers was simply the idea of robots that could change into other things, like cars, planes, and guns. But that was the conceit behind the cobbled-together *toy line*, not the *story* of the Transformers. By the time the Transformers got to the public as a *story*, on TV and in Marvel Comics, it by necessity had a very different conceit: the Transformers were aliens, divided into two warring factions, whose war had (by chance) come to Earth.

It was a basic conceit. At their worst, early Transformers stories simply used this as a backstory to justify robots fighting each other, with Cybertron mostly relevant as a convenient place from which to introduce new characters.

But in the best Transformers stories, and the best *parts* of Transformers stories, there were suggestions that these aliens were, in fact, well and truly *alien*.

After all, we're talking about *mechanical life*. Something very alien from us. Yes, it's cool that they transform — although I wanted to know how this developed. But it seemed obvious to me that the even more important difference was that these aliens were *made of metal* — presumably a precondition for transforming.

Usually, artists of both the cartoon and the comic would depict the Transformers on Cybertron — those who had never, or hadn't *yet*, copied human mechanical forms — rather unimaginatively, with only slight variations on Earth-bound designs. But on the cartoon show, there were the Decepticon jets, depicted in their Cybertronian forms more like stylized versions of flying four-sided dice. It was a small touch, to be sure, but it suggested at least that vehicles on Cybertron wouldn't look like those on Earth. Then there was the design of Cybertron, with huge holes running through the planet and elevated platforms instead of roads. As the cartoon progressed, we also got glimpses of Cybertron's past, including Optimus Prime's predecessors as Autobot leader.

The comics were slightly more ambitious. Few comics have influenced me more than *Transformers* #1 (Sept 1984). Partly due to penciler Frank Springer following the toy designs a bit slavishly so early in the series, the characters looked clunky and less humanoid. Some even seemed to lack heads. In fact, we see versions of Ratchet and Ironhide that — like their toys — literally lacked heads and chests, resembling more what robots might actually look like. I've always loved these — and the U.K.'s — very earliest comics for this reason, among others. Yes, the robots might look clunky, but at least they don't look like they were engineered to look humanoid without looking like humanesque androids.

Rereading *Transformers* #1 as a child, I inevitably found myself thinking about the Transformers' origins. Given that Cybertron seemed so dominated by metals, I concluded that silicon-based life had evolved there naturally. There was a whole Transformers evolutionary history in my mind, leading towards specialization that in time created the Autobot / Decepticon division. Later, after the 1986 movie, both the comic and the cartoon would (to my disappointment) establish different origins for the Transformers (the Quintessons and Primus, respectively), avoiding my (more interesting, I think) evolutionary explanation. But that far more alien, evolutionary explanation had come from hints in the comic themselves, which suggested a truly *alien* planet with its own culture and history.

Another charming aspect of these stories was that the Transformers initially tried to speak to cars, unaware that they weren't alive. But there was a scene in *Transformers* #1 that suggested that the Ark — the Autobots' crashed spaceship — perceived vehicles as the planet's dominant lifeform. Even my child mind realized that, viewed from an alien perspective, it could easily look like humans serviced their cars, around which society was organized, rather than the other way around. Again, my brain might have gone to a more alien possibility, but it was a potential hinted at in the stories themselves.

As the comics progressed, we learned that Optimus Prime possessed something called the Matrix, which originally allowed for the creation of new Transformers life, while residing in his program rather than in his chest cavity. This didn't *really* make sense. Why couldn't Optimus Prime's code be copied, duplicating the Matrix? How did the Decepticons — who sometimes seemed to outnumbered the Autobots — generate new beings? And how did Transformers who were "really" alive differ from very complex robots? Wasn't this — and the irreproducable nature of Transformers' programming — a bit of mysticism suggesting a soul? This stuff irritated me, even as a child. But at least in the comics, the Matrix began to explain how the Transformers reproduced — even if it raised more questions than answers.

Transformers: The Movie borrowed the idea of the Matrix from the comics, but transformed it into a device stored in Optimus Prime's chest. Apparently, all Autobots — or only all potential Autobot leaders — were built with a similar chest cavity, allowing them to incorporate the Matrix if need be. It was treated as a one-of-a-kind religious object, and it was the subject of a prophecy that it someday "the Chosen One" would arise and use the Matrix to "light [the Autobots'] darkest hour." By the end of the movie, we see this apparently ages-old prophecy fulfilled, when Hot Rod becomes Rodimus Prime and opens the Matrix, destroying Unicron.

Sure, this was a retcon. Everyone — Autobots and Decepticons — knew all about the Matrix, yet it had never been mentioned before in the cartoon.

Still, even a child like I was would recognize that the Matrix prophecy was a messiah story. *The Transformers had a religion*.

This fascinated me. It may have only been in the movie to service the movie's plot — it was certainly convenient that the Matrix could so quickly destroy the otherwise unbeatable Unicron. But my mind *loved* the idea that the alien Transformers would have an alien religion.

Star Wars got an absurd amount of praise for depicting a sci-fi religion, even if it wasn't much more complicated than that of *Transformers: The Movie*. But most depictions of aliens didn't have much in the way of religion. Years later, the rebooted *Battlestar Galactica* got a lot of mileage out of the religious differences between the humans and the artificial Cylons.

Even at eight, I felt like the introduction of religion into the Transformers story was a step in the right direction — a move towards finally exploring the obvious alien implications that had been a part of the Transformers all along.

While we're on the topic of how *Transformers: The Movie* seemed a step in the right direction, it also appeared to authenticate my evolutionary theory of the mechanical Transformers' origins. The brilliant opening of *Transformers: The Movie* featured an entirely *different* planet dominated by mechanical life, without any suggestion of a shared origin with the Transformers. Unicron, the planet-devouring villain of the movie, further suggested this. The implication, for me, was that silicon-based life evolves often enough in the galaxy — and may even be more common than carbon-based life. This was something I wanted the series to continue to explore!

Sadly, the Transformers franchise never really followed through on all these implications, which I rather foolishly assumed were matters that *must* have been discussed by the writing staff all along — rather than conveniences of a specific plot, later embellished or ignored by the short-term needs of subsequent plots.

In fairness, the Matrix did get further explored on the third season of the cartoon show, which took place in 2006, following the events of the movie. Now, it was revealed that the Matrix contained the accumulated wisdom of all past Autobot leaders, as well as those leaders themselves. (Apparently, when they died, they went inside the Matrix as they passed it to their successor?)

While hokey in its execution, this idea of a repository of information, or of (at least some) Transformers effectively having an afterlife, did expand the religious concept. The idea of mechanical life escaping death did further hint at the differences between the alien Transformers and organic life — another difference the revived *Battlestar Galactica* explored to some critical acclaim.

But as previously mentioned, some of these same episodes of the cartoon revealed that the Transformers had been created by the organic Quintessons. I appreciated an exploration of the Transformers' origins, as well as how *weird* the Quintessons were. But this explanation did root the Transformers' mechanical life in an organic origin, which took away from the uniqueness of the concept.

Personally, I regard the comics explanation of the Transformers origin — in which Unicron and Primus were Manichean entities — as less satisfying (despite my respect for Transformers comics writer Simon Furman).

By far, the cartoon's greatest failure was its inability to follow through on the concept of Rodimus Prime as messiah. This was "the Chosen One," after all. This didn't prevent further conflict; the Autobots might have regained Cybertron during the movie, but the Decepticons and Quintessons could always be used to drive a plot. Yet the cartoon's writers failed to adequately dramatize Rodimus Prime's difficulties in being an actual messiah, while having no real leadership experience. Such stories would inevitably be difficult to write, since they'd have to keep Rodimus Prime a legitimate messiah, without looking pathetically insecure, while also dramatizing his inner conflict and odd situation. The result was a character who alternated between extreme insecurity and boring uprightness — and who certainly seemed like a poor substitution for the beloved Optimus Prime. Optimus returned from the dead at the end of the third season, at which point "the Chosen One" handed over the Matrix without a single word of protest.

So much for the messiah. You can create one easily enough, but there aren't a lot of models to draw upon for following through on his story.

The cartoon didn't last much longer. The comic outlived the cartoon, coming to an end in 1991. The Transformers have gone through many iterations since, which have made alterations and improvements to the Transformers formula. But they haven't fully lived up to the promise and intellectual possibilities suggested by *Transformers: The Movie*.

You can improve upon animation quality, or plenty of other more superficial aspects. You can also craft a plot that avoids some of the problems of *Transformers: The Movie* — although, if Transformers history is an guide, you're likely to create new problems. But it's hard to beat the newness and sheer sense of possibility of *Transformers: The Movie*.[*]

---

[*] First published on Sequart Organization's website in June 2014.

Unicron Vs. Galactus:
Battle of the Planet-Eaters!

When coming up with villains, you usually want someone who poses a real threat to the story's heroes. Few things are as important to a story as making the conflict seem like something's at stake. But if you make a villain or the threat too strong, it can become too abstract or nebulous.

Most villains are roughly as powerful as the hero. If your hero is a spy or a martial artist, the villain may well be a spy or a martial artist. Many of the best villains are the evil equivalents of their heroes — Zod to Superman, Prometheus to Batman — and there's a special satisfaction to this kind of pairing.

Sometimes, a villain is weaker than the hero. This was often the case in classic super-hero stories, with their Captain Boomerangs and Stilt-Mans. Sometimes the best pairings are mismatched, like a strong hero against a smart villain, or vice versa.

Of course, many of the best villains are more powerful than the hero. That's why the Kingpin works as a Daredevil villain, because the Kingpin isn't simply strong; he's the wealthy boss of a criminal empire.

One of the more interesting aspects of the Transformers — though sadly rarely explored — is that the Autobots were implicitly the underdogs. They transformed into *cars*. But the Decepticons transformed into *weapons*. Sure, the Autobots won, again and again. But by their very nature, the Decepticons had the upper hand.

But we're still talking about pairings on roughly the same level. Let's get a little more creative here.

The Kardashev scale is a way of measuring hypothetical civilizations. A Type I civilization is capable of utilizing all of the resources of its planet. A Type II, its star. A Type III, its galaxy. Some have proposed a Type IV, which can control its universe, or a Type V, which can control multiple universes. We're still a Type 0 civilization.

Some villains are so strong that they register on the Kardashev scale.

In super-hero comics, there's an odd and unsatisfying tendency to jump from Type 0 – such as the villains discussed above – to Type IV. Villains are so often remaking the entire universe. The Anti-Monitor was a Type V villain, unmaking DC's multiverse. Thanos, with the Infinity Guantlet, was a Type IV. Hal Jordan, in *Zero Hour*, was a Type IV villain (since he was only unmaking a single universe, the DC multiverse having been condensed to a single universe). Again and again, we hear of unmaking existence... as if that could be anything but an abstract threat. Yet there's an odd lack of middle ground, between Type 0 and Types IV-V. This oddity is even stranger when you consider how bizarre it is that someone with recognizably human patterns of thought and motivation could ever achieve a Type IV level of power... let alone leap to this level directly from Type 0.

A few examples do occupy this middle ground. There's the Sun-Eater, from Legion of Super-Heroes – although he's usually depicted as instinctive and thus isn't much of a villain per se. The Death Star's a Type I menace, capable of blowing up planets with a single blast.

Type I and Type II villains offer plenty of cosmic threat. There's no need to go beyond this, and doing so tends to make the already mind-boggling threat feel oddly impotent. Imagine if the Death Star could blast whole galaxies apart. How would we even process that, as readers?

Of the Type I villains, two of the most classic are planet-eaters: Galactus and Unicron.

It's said that when Jack Kirby and Stan Lee, in 1966, created Galactus as a foe for the Fantastic Four, their idea was to up the ante by having the super-hero team battle a god. It's telling that they didn't create a Type IV (or Type V) villain, which would be closer to a monotheistic creator-god. Instead, they came up with a giant purple humanoid alien with Caucasian skin and (originally) a big "G" on his chest.

Galactus doesn't *literally* eat planets. Instead, he sets up giant alien machinery that sucks the "life force" out of planets, killing everything on them and leaving them barren.

Of course, the Fantastic Four defeated Galactus, and it took years before comics took advantage of the obvious drama of depicting Galactus actually successfully consuming a planet. (The first full-length depiction of this occurred in *Galactus the Devourer* #1, Sept 1999.)

Among superhero comics fans, Galactus is often revered – largely because a planet-eating was such a cool. But as a planet-eater, he left much to be desired. His anthropomorphism let readers comprehend him as a threat, but it also made him seem more than a little ridiculous in retrospect.

So when it came time to update Galactus for Marvel's Ultimate Universe (in the 2004-2006 Ultimate Galactus trilogy), writer Warren Ellis stripped the planet-eater of his absurd anthropomorphic aspects. This new Galactus, called Gah Lak Tus, was a swarm of mechanical devices with a collective mind. While this version deprived readers of a giant humanoid villain, rendering the planet-eater more abstract, this new Galactus wasn't *so* abstract that it wasn't dramatic. Indeed, there was something frightening in its cold-minded practicality and technological realism... even if it didn't make as good a visual.

The 2007 film *Fantastic Four: Rise of the Silver Surfer* took a less successful path, reimagining Galactus as a kind of cosmic cloud. This avoided the anthropomorphism of the original, which would have been hard to depict convincingly in film, yet was far more abstract and less successful than Ultimate Galactus.

But before either of these reimaginings, 1986's *Transformers: The Movie* offered a rival planet-eater in Unicron.

Unlike Galactus, this version wasn't humanoid. Instead, it looked like a ringed mechanical moon, or a small planet, with a giant maw.

And it didn't use weird technology to suck the life force out of a planet, like some kind of cosmic vampire. No, Unicron ate a planet literally.

Of course, there's a reason for this: Unicron was probably more directly inspired by the Death Star than by Galactus. Much of the animated movie shows a Star Wars influence, right down to Arcee's head shape, which echoes Princess Leia's side buns. But Unicron devoured planets, not blasted them, making him functionally closer to Galactus than to the Death Star.

Long before the first convincing depiction of Galactus successfully devouring a planet, *Transformers: The Movie* opened with a mostly silent sequence in which we see a planet, Lithone, buzzing with mechanical lifeforms – all of which is consumed by Unicron. We watch as characters try to flee, only to get sucked into the villain along with the rest of their civilization.

Unicron devours Lithone, from the beginning of *Transformers: The Movie.*

Moreover, we follow the pieces of the planet into Unicron, where we see this planet-devourer's *digestion process*. Chunks of the planet — and its inhabitants — get metabolized. At the end of the sequence, we watch as resulting energy flows through Unicron, rippling out to the planet-eater's rings. We then pull back and watch as it floats off, through the empty space where a planet and an entire civilization once was.

It's a great way of establishing Unicron's threat. In fact, it's probably one of the most dramatic openings to a story *ever*.

Unicron's established before any of the other Transformers. And the first thing we see him do is destroy *and metabolize* an entire planet.

It's not too much to say that this opening sequence out-does the best Galactus sequence. It's that good.

As a Type I villain, Unicron avoids the anthropocentrism of Galactus, yet manages to be even *more* menacing. Unicron's mouth gives the viewer its only anthropocentric element, and even that's closer to a leech's mouth than a human one. And how poetic is it that the one identifiable animalistic feature of Unicron's design is his *mouth*? The effect is to make Unicron seem less human and more like a force of nature.

But while Unicron solves the problem of Galactus's anthropocentrism, Unicron offers a far more imposing visual than either Ultimate Galactus or the 2007 movie Galactus.

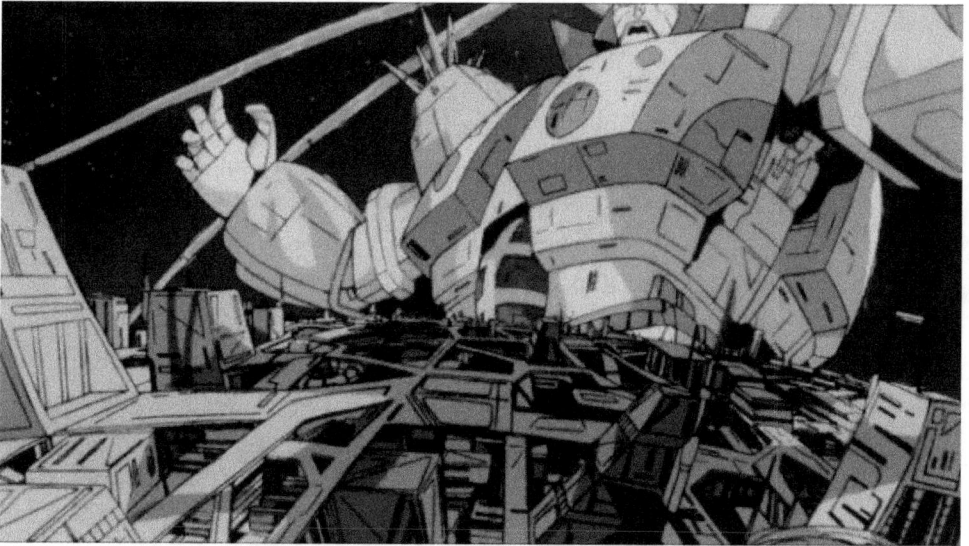

Unicron tears through Cybertron, in the climax of *Transformers: The Movie*.

The parallels between Galactus and Unicron go far beyond the fact that both eat planets. Both have "heralds," human-size minions who go ahead of their larger bosses. Galactus had the Silver Surfer (and later, many, many others), while Unicron had Galvatron, Cyclonus, Scourge, and a small army of clones. Without denigrating the Silver Surfer, it's hard to beat a more vicious incarnation of the franchise's main villain.

One of the problems of villains who register on the Kardashev scale is that it's hard to come up with a way to defeat them. The likelihood of a *deus ex machina* resolution increases proportionately with the villain's threat.

That's the case with Galactus's first appearance, in which the Fantastic Four defeats Galactus with a tiny, hand-held device called the Ultimate Nullifier. As silly as Galactus can be, the Ultimate Nullifier is worse.

Transformers: The Movie is a little better, in that the mystical Matrix is established almost from the beginning. But still, once the Matrix is opened (or activated), it blows up Unicron, as if it's automatic.

Another problem the two villains share is that they've been the subject of some rather silly revisions over time. Part of the reason for this is an obvious limitation in human thinking. Logically, a Type I villain is simply a planet-eater and has no deeper connection with the universe or with reality than any planet would. But the human mind isn't built to imagine Type I concerns. It's far too easy for a Type I villain to slide mentally into a Type IV villain, or to acquire Type IV attributes.

So Galactus has been retconned to be an explorer from a universe that preceded the Big Bang, who survived his universe's destruction, somehow bonded with our universe's essence and gestated until he took the form with which we're familiar. It's an absurd origin, especially since it's hard to imagine anything connected with the universe being only slighter larger than a human or an ant, at least compared with the vastness of galactic clusters. Again and again, Galactus has been treated as a mystical force, important not only to Type I concerns but to the entire universe.

Similarly, Unicron was retconned to be the embodiment of Chaos whose origins go back to the beginning of the universe. His twin, Primus, the incarnation of Order, is the originator of the Transformers. Supposedly, only one copy of Unicron and Primus exist in the entire multiverse, to which they're said to be essential. This would make Unicron a Type V villain.

It's easy to see where these changes originate. It's tempting to want to add importance to a successful villain (especially one rarely used), and it's easy to add Type IV traits to a Type I character, considering both are equally unimaginable from a human perspective. Still, it's absurd to think that anything important to the structure of the universe would be planet-sized (or far less, in the case of Galactus), nor preoccupied with eating something so *small*, nor recognizably good or evil.

But this does illustrate the clear difficulties of even imagining villains on this scale. But as the popularity of both Unicron and Galactus illustrate, the rewards for success can be great too.[*]

---

[*] First published on Sequart Organization's website in June 2014.

When the Good Guys Deserted:
On the Blaster Saga

In 1986's *Transformers: The Movie*, set in 2005, both the Autobots and Decepticons got new leaders. Marvel Comics adapted the movie as a three-issue mini-series, but the main comic book (at least in the U.S.) ostensibly ignored those events. The series didn't leap forward to 2006, the way the cartoon show did after the movie. Instead, the Marvel series, written by Bob Budiansky, continued in the present, ignoring the new characters introduced in the movie.

Despite this, the ongoing Marvel comic oddly mirrored the movie by killing off (in issue #24, Jan 1987) the Autobots' leader, Optimus Prime – and in the very next issue (#25, Feb 1987), the Decepticons' leader, Megatron. Both died in very different circumstances from their movie deaths — circumstances that were fascinatingly low-key, compared to the movie's epic battles. Both issues are now considered classics.

Perhaps even more amazing, the story depicting Megatron's death didn't feature the Autobots; it was an all-Decepticon issue, an idea far ahead of its time in 1986. The next issue (#26, Mar 1987) reversed this formula, focusing on the Autobots and centered around Optimus Prime's funeral. The next issue (#27, Apr 1987) occurred while the Autobots struggled to choose a new leader. Grimlock, the leader of the Dinobots known for his mix of stupidity and braggadocio, demanded to be chosen. It seemed — to the Autobots, as well as to readers — like an absurd suggestion. But by the end of the story, Grimlock proved himself, even acting humble in the aftermath, and was indeed chosen to lead the Autobots.

It's hard to describe just how shocking these four issues were. They proceeded methodically, totally upending the status quo of the series. That was Bob Budiansky's intent; he later explained that many of his decisions on the title during this period were based on making choices that would be unexpected or shocking. And he certainly succeeded with these four issues.

While those four issues are best thought of as a unit, they did continue some plots left over from previous issues. And they occurred concurrently with the four-issue *G.I. Joe and the Transformers* mini-series, written by Michael Higgins. The four issues of that mini-series make explicit references to the events of these four issues of the regular Transformers series, and the eight issues really work together as a block — that systematically changes the status quo of the Transformers series while weaving in and out of an extended story featuring G.I. Joe and Cobra.

Of course, such radical changes to the status quo, while exciting, also present narrative challenges. Shocking developments are one thing, but turning them into compelling stories is quite another. And that's the mark of a real writer.

That's also where Budiansky succeeded, crafting a saga that was among the very best in the original comic's history.

Transformers stories tend to feature an ensemble cast. That's true of many series featuring teams. But the Transformers comic (and the G.I. Joe one), new toys were being introduced all the time, and the comic had to incorporate them. This meant that the title's ensemble cast was perpetually growing, and the need to focus on new characters made it difficult to develop any characters in any depth or to tell extended storylines.

To address this, Budiansky would focus on two Autobots — Blaster and Goldbug — who fled the rest of the Autobots, now ruled by Grimlock. New characters would still be introduced, but they would be woven into the ongoing story of Blaster and Goldbug. (Goldbug was actually the same Autobot as Bumblebee, who had been destroyed and rebuilt during *G.I. Joe and the Transformers* — and given a new name for the occasion. This reflected the fact that the Goldbug toy was a car that looked very much like a gold Volkswagen beetle, which was very similar to Bumblebee's original design as a yellow beetle.) The emphasis on Blaster and Goldbug let the comic tell an ongoing story, focused on a few characters. But the effect of this was to decentralize the Autobots at large from what used to be *their* comic. Blaster and Goldbug were now the stars, and the Autobots were now recast as the villains — or *one* set of villains, since the more overtly evil Decepticons were still present as antagonists.

There's probably no more central conceit to the Transformers than that the Autobots are the good guys and the Decepticons the bad guys. Budiansky was about to upend that too.

Many Transformers stories have focused on crises of leadership. The Decepticons have often been depicted as having multiple characters interested in seizing command. With the Autobots, story after story has focused on the burden of command, as characters — usually Optimus Prime, though not always — struggle with the casualties and other consequences of their decisions. To the credit of Transformers stories, this kind of moral wrestling and self-doubt is usually depicted as the sign of a good leader who takes his job seriously. But most stories depict Autobot leaders, especially Optimus Prime, as unquestionably right and noble. Optimus Prime might rule the Autobots like an authoritarian monarch, but he's consistently a benevolent one, who makes mistakes but takes accountability for them.

While this provides a positive example of what good leadership means, it's not without its problems. Because a king is still a king. Optimus Prime might be an excellent leader, but the underlying structure of Autobot authority is a dangerous one. The problem with benevolent dictators, no matter how efficient or how seductive an idea, is that such a government is ultimately responsible to the dictator's whims. And there's always a next guy. Even the best emperor can be followed by a bad one, who can use the same structure of unchecked authority to take whole societies down catastrophic and self-destructive paths.

That's what the saga Budiansky crafted explored. He may have intended simply to write a surprising story, or to take the Transformers in a new direction. But the result was an interrogation of power... and of why loyalty is owed when you think your nation is still the good guys, relatively speaking, but is doing terribly misguided and even wrong things.

The new storyline began with the very next issue, following Grimlock becoming the Autobots' leader. When we first see him in issue #28 (May 1987) — penciled by Don Perlin and inked by Ian

Akin & Brian Garvey — he's fitting himself for a crown to reflect his new status. The humility Grimlock found, at the end of the previous issue, seems to have been a passing fancy, and it's clear that things are very, very wrong. Blaster and Goldbug appear scared to tell Grimlock displeasing news, and they have reason to seem intimidated: Grimlock smashes things in frustration, then asks angrily why Blaster and Goldbug didn't simply *kill* the humans who interfered with their mission, rather than abort that mission.

Grimlock fits himself for a crown. From *Transformers* #28 (May 1987).

Grimlock soon sends Blaster and Goldbug back out on a mission, promising punishment if they fail. That mission occupies most of the issue, and it's not particularly memorable. What *is* remarkable is how miserable Blaster and Goldbug are. Instead of killing the humans, they cooperate, and they're victorious. But they haven't achieved the mission's goals, and they know Grimlock — whom they don't respect — won't be happy. So in the final panels, they decide to drive *away* from the Ark, the Autobots' base.

If the Transformers are soldiers in a civil war, Blaster and Goldbug have gone AWOL — absent without leave. They're deserters.

Moreover, they've disobeyed orders. Yes, those were immoral orders – to kill any humans who got in their way. If Blaster and Goldbug were human soldiers, this would be an illegal order, under international law. But it's still disobeying the orders of a military superior.

But in the great tradition of morality tales, we identify with them.

Decrying their leader, Blaster and Goldbug head away from the Ark, in the conclusion of *Transformers* #28 (May 1987).

The Transformers comic routinely featured dangling plotlines, and there was no guarantee that Blaster and Goldbug would be the focus of the following issues. But they were. And although one would expect that this would be difficult to write, the result was a two-part story that's considered one of the best in Transformers history.

"Crater Critters" (issue #29, June 1987) — also illustrated by Perlin, Akin, and Garvey — begins dramatically, with what might be a meteor crashing into the American Southwest. But it's not a meteor; it's a spacecraft. Out of the crater, a battered, dying Transformer's hand reaches out, but he can't lift himself free, and he slides back inside.

Blaster and Goldbug check in on oil baron G.B. Blackrock, who'd been shown in previous issues. Hearing their story, Blackrock is the first to call them *"deserters."* The two Autobots are interested in news of Decepticon activity. Apparently, despite their desertion, they're eager to continue the war with the Decepticons. Blackrock informs them of the apparent spacecraft crash, and the two Autobots head toward the site.

On Cybertron, we learn that the ship that crashed was sent by the Decepticon Ratbat. Making Ratbat one of the Decepticon leaders was another one of Budiansky's surprising moves: Ratbat was one of the Decepticon cassettes and therefore one of the most minor of all the Transformers toys. Essentially, he was an accessory to Soundwave, the Decepticon who transformed into a cassette tape player. (Remember, this was the 1980s.) Ratbat didn't even have a proper robot form; he was a mechanical bat who transformed into a cassette tape. His toy wasn't even sold on its own; instead, it was packaged with another Decepticon cassette. As Budiansky intended, making Raybat the apparent leader of the Decepticons on Cybertron was more than unexpected. It went against how the largest and most expensive toys were supposed to be the most important, but it also suggested that size needn't matter quite so much. After all, these were mechanical life forms, and there was no need for the best brains (or the best programming?) to be in the physically largest bodies.

Ratbat sends the three Decepticon triple-changes (Astrotrain, Blitzwing, and Octane) to investigate. (Remember when I said that, even during this storyline, the comic would have to introduce new characters?) They arrive at the crash site, chase some human scientists away, and begin their investigation with typical Decepticon arrogance. The survivor seen earlier warns them to stay away, but they don't listen, and they're soon infected by what took down the craft.

Blaster and Goldbug enlist a scientist named Charlie Fong to help them get past the site's military guards. Fong's a typical Autobot-helping human character, but it's notable that he's Asian. The story plays this with a pretty soft touch; his ethnicity isn't a huge point. But an army lieutenant does get a panel of thought balloons, remarking on Fong's bravery: "That little guy must be the bravest man I ever met," the soldier thinks, adding, "Who'd have guessed?" As a kid, I wouldn't have picked up on the fact that this soldier's thoughts were racial. But as an adult, I can appreciate the fact that the comic was trying to be diverse and to portray an Asian character in a positive light — without being too overt or preachy about it.

As Blaster engages the three Decepticon triple-changers, Goldbug and Fong question the ship's pilot. The infection that downed the ship is caused by tiny Transformers — so small that they transform into nuts and bolts — called Scraplets. It's a fascinating idea, rooted in the fact that the Transformers turn into metal objects. What kind of Transformer might transform into into something as small as a screw? A Transformers virus — another fascinating idea. A lot of the best Transformers stories revolve around exploring implications of them being mechanical life, such as their religion or origins or diseases, and this story is no exception.

Hearing about the Scraplets, Blaster explains that he's heard of them: "They evolved the ability to resemble harmless nuts, bolts, screws[,] and the like... but they're supposed to be the *deadliest disease known* to mechanical life forms in the entire galaxy!" It's a slightly ham-fisted bit of dialogue, but it does its job of selling both the idea of the Scraplets and their threat. It also suggests that the Scraplets, though not necessarily *all* Transformers, *evolved*, and it further alludes to the idea that the Transformers are aware of other forms of "mechanical life" in the universe (something the opening of *Transformers: The Movie* suggests).

As the story nears its conclusion, Blaster radios Goldbug for help, but Goldbug — convinced that finding a cure must be the top priority — abandons Blaster. Goldbug wrestles with the decision, and Blaster rages angrily at what he considers Goldbug's cowardice. But Goldbug's situation reflects the need for tough decisions, in times of war or outbreak — something Blaster's referenced earlier in the story. Goldbug's choice to abandon Blaster also echoes their decision, at the end of the previous issue, to abandon the other Autobots. I don't think readers could suspect that Blaster's correct and that Goldbug's a coward, but it's hard to miss that these two deserters seem to have deserted one another in the very next episode. Without making this too obvious, the story puts Blaster and Goldbug under extreme circumstances in order to test whether these two deserters can remain loyal to one another... or whether their splinter group of two will rapidly fall apart.

Goldbug drives away from the crash site, but not before he's infected by a single, stray Scraplet. It soon reproduces in Goldbug's "skin," and Fong is unable to remove it. As Goldbug drives, he deteriorates rapidly. Don Perlin and his inkers depict this rather brilliantly, and it's amazing how unsettling it is to see Goldbug with holes in his hood and his bumper falling off. Goldbug seems on the verge of death — a situation made all the more dramatic because he seems to have abandoned Blaster for nothing. Goldbug pleads: "Charlie... you can't let me *die* here... not with Blaster *needing* me... thinking I *betrayed* him... you can't...!"

It's a great cliffhanger, but it gets a great deal of its dramatic tension from the way it tests these two deserters in that context.

Issue #30 (July 1987) – also by Budiansky, Perlin, Akin, and Garvey – continues the story, but begins in an unorthodox fashion: by introducing the Throttlebots on Cybertron. The Throttlebots were small Transformers toys that, when pulled backwards, drove forward on their own. In fact, Goldbug was part of this line of toys. Typically, a group such as this would have been introduced all together in the comics, but Goldbug's similarity to Bumblebee led to his introduction first. The Throttlebots would be the second group of characters whose introduction was woven into the saga of Blaster and Goldbug's treason, and their introduction helped solve the seeminglessly hopeless cliffhanger of the previous issue.

The Throttlebots are captured on Cybertron and taken to Ratbat, who updates us about the situation in the crater. The

Decepticons Ratbat sent have captured Blaster, but they're all weakening due to the Scraplet infection. Ratbat says he's "unwilling to risk the lives of any more Decepticons," and so he's sending the captured Throttlebots — to sanitize the Scraplet infection, killing all those infected.

On Earth, Charlie Fong is now pushing the dying Goldbug... but finds a gas station over a desert ridge. Charlie's dying of thirst, so he gets a drink of water. When he spills some on Goldbug, the Scraplets where the water landed fall off. Yes, the cure is water — which invites unflattering comparisons to *The Wizard of Oz*. This is slightly redeemed by the fact that there's been allusion to a cure multiple times in the story, but it's said to be an extremely rare chemical. Implicitly, there's no water on Cybertron — another sign that mechanical life evolved there, rather than was built by organic beings (who would have needed water). But there's a twist: this is the desert, after all, and the gas station attendants stop Charlie's attempt to wash his car. All the water's "trucked in," and given the state Goldbug's in, they suggest junking the car instead.

The Throttlebots arrive at the crater, where the Decepticons recognize them as Autobots but are too weak to attack. In a nice little sequence, a dying Blitzwing crashes into the side of the crater, and Scraplets leap off of him, transform, and head towards the new food that's arrived. It's pretty cool to think of a sentient virus like this, and it's also noteworthy that the Scraplets' word balloons have geometric shapes, reminiscent of their alternate forms as nuts and bolts. It's a minor touch by letterer Janice Chiang, but it was done here years before different styles of word balloons to reflect specific characters became popularized (on titles such as Neil Gaiman's *The Sandman*).

The Throttlebots notice the tracks Goldbug left, when fled last issue, and send a couple of the Throttlebots after them, intent on eliminating the Scraplet infection. They find the decrepit Goldbug at the gas station, where Charlie's been unable to secure a car wash. They fight the weakened Goldbug a bit before Charlie throws some Scraplets onto one of the Throttlebots, then cures him with some water.

Goldbug then calls G.B. Blackrock, who was seen in the previous issue, and gets him to deliver a couple tankers of water to the crater. But Blaster refuses to be cured, since this would mean the Decepticons would be cured too. He *really* hates Decepticons, apparently. Goldbug concedes and tells the Throttlebots to use the acid they've prepared, instead of the water.

The Scraplets leap off a dying Blitzwing in *Transformers* #30 (July 1987).

But the Scraplets merge to form one giant creature. Yes, having little things combine into one giant monster (that somehow seems to have a single consciousness) is a cliché, but it's still fun. Since Ratbat sent the Throttlebots to Earth without weapons (not wanting to arm Autobots), Goldbug's forced to cure the armed Transformers in the crater, who then defeat the Scraplet monster. The

Decepticons then fly off with the contents of the crashed ship — which are revealed in the following issue.

It's a classic two-part story, and the Scraplets have gone on to become part of Transformers lore (even if the cool implications about Transformers evolution haven't stuck). But as entertaining as the story is, it's also a kind of test case for the two deserters. When they reconcile, at the end of the issue, it's a traditional happy ending, but it's also the proof that the schism between these deserters and the rest of the Autobots isn't due to some personality defect in those deserters. They won't turn against each other too. In fact, they've expanded, adding the Throttlebots to their group.

The next issue (#31, Aug 1987) — by Budianski and Perlin, with finished art by Jim Fern — takes a break from the Blaster and Goldbug story, but it ties into Ratbat's plan with the crashed ship. Entitled "Buster Witwicky and the Car Wash of Doom," it's a charmingly hokey story, in which Ratbat uses a chain of car washes (and G.B. Blackrock, who became mind-controlled in the previous issue) to brainwash humans into letting the Decepticons siphon the human vehicles' fuel. The story's a nice, campy break from the Blaster and Goldbug story. Buster Witwicky was once a big part of the series (in the early issues), so it's nice to see him (along with his girlfriend) get a starring role, and the highlight of the issue is Ratbat, especially when he attacks Buster inside a car wash.

When we rejoin the Blaster and Goldbug plot — in issue #32 (Sept 1987), by Budiansky, Perkin, Akin, and Garvey —they're travelling with the (rest of the) Throttlebots and being menaced by both the Decepticons and R.A.A.T., a military organization tasked with eliminating the Transformers threat. While the cartoon and most of the later Transformers continuities had Earth quickly learn the difference between the Autobots and Decepticons, this distinction wasn't known in any widespread way in the comic book. R.A.A.T. isn't the most subtle of acronyms, but it worked as a paramilitary organization in line with Marvel's S.H.I.E.L.D. or with G.I. Joe — although, of course, placed in the position of being a villain.

After the fight with R.A.A.T., we see Grimlock for the first time since Blaster and Goldbug defected. He's just as arrogant as be was then. Having heard of Blaster's battle with R.A.A.T., he orders the Protectobots – a team of combiners (Transformers who could unite to form a giant robot, called a "gestalt" form by many Transformers fans) organized around the "rescue" theme (a police car, a fire truck, an ambulance, etc.) – to retrieve Blaster and Goldbug. The sequence is only a page, demonstrating how truly decentered the series had become from the Autobots in the Ark, which had always been the main contingent of Autobots on Earth.

Having driven through the night after the R.A.A.T. battle, Blaster and the Throttlebots decide to lay low during the day, hiding in a used car lot. It's just the kind of quaint plot at which Budiansky often excelled. As soon as the Autobots have settled in, the plot turns to focus on Big Steve, the proprietor of the used car lot. He's a clichéd used car salesman, who are conventionally depicted as thoroughly unethical, but he's a lot of fun to watch conning unsuspecting customers. When he discovers the Throttlebots, he doesn't ask any questions and is only too glad to make plans to sell them. When the Throttlebots transform, Big Steve at first assumes they're from the Better Business Bureau. He promises to give them fuel and stay the night, but he promptly turns them in for a reward and sabotages the fuel he gives them.

R.A.A.T. arrives, but the Throttlebots find that they can't transform – thanks to the poisoned fuel. The Combaticons – the Decepticon opposite of the Protectobots – also arrive, as do the Protectobots. With a fight brewing, Big Steve suggests settling who gets the Throttlebots through an auction (which he'll reap the proceeds from), instead of an conflict (which would trash his used car lot). One of the Combaticons readies a cannon to kill Big Steve, but Blaster intervenes. With conflict about to break out, R.A.A.T. hands Big Steve a check and tells him to get out of the way.

The fight that follows is pretty rote – and it's not easy to guess that Budiansky had to shoehorn the Protectobots and Combaticons into the plot. What's most remarkably are Big Steve's moments, providing some side comedy during the fighting. In one panel, we see a car that's torn to shreds but still bears the sign "Like New Only $2100.00." Steve, hiding behind the car, says, "M-maybe I should offer a discount on this one…" When a Transformer falls on a car, tearing it apart, Steve pounds his fists in frustration, saying, "No! I already *sold* that Buick – / – for *triple* what it was worth!"

During the fight, R.A.A.T. loads the helpless Throttlebots and flees. The battle turns when Blaster joins his fellow Autobots, and the Combaticons soon flee. The issue's conclusion then offers two twists. First, Steve looks at his ruined used car lot, only to greedily grasp his check — which Blaster disintegrates. Blaster has saved Steve's life, but he doesn't think Steve should profit from Blaster losing his friends, the Throttlebots. It's a nice conclusion to Steve's brief arc, and a comeuppance readers can enjoy. In the second twist, Blaster prepares the Protectobots to go after R.A.A.T. — only to have the Protectobots level their guns on him.

The Protectobots take Blaster into custody, in the twist climax of *Transformers* #32 (Sept 1987).

"Grimlock didn't send us here to *rescue* you," says Hotspot, the leader of the Protectobots. "He sent us here to *arrest* you for rebelling against his command... / ...and to bring you back to the Ark for *trial* and *execution!*"

It's a great, pulpy cliffhanger, and it's the first moment that the story of these deserters positions Autobot against Autobot. This wasn't the first time any Autobot fought another Autobot. For example, the conclusion of the first year of the title (#12, Jan 1986) saw the Autobots battle a mind-controlled Optimus Prime. But this was probably the first time Autobots were consciously and deliberately taking arms against one another.

There's an extra irony here in that the Autobots raising their weapons − and promising Blaster's execution − are named the Protectobots. They might be rescue vehicles, but there's not acting as rescuers. They're acting as soldiers, following orders to take action against a deserter. And while that's logical, it upsets the traditional notion of the Autobots as protectors and as the good guys. Are they moral heroes, or are they ultimately soldiers too? And if they're the latter, the difference between the two factions becomes far less black and white.

From a narrative standpoint, it's worth noting that Big Steve has just received his comeuppance from Blaster when the Protectobots raise their guns. The Protectobots only won due to Blaster's interference, and Blaster's intervention in the battle begins by saving Hotspot from being shot in the back. When Hotspot returns the favor by arresting Blaster, it's hard not to feel that he's ungrateful... even if he is following orders.

But as Big Steve asserts when he loses his check, life's not fair. "I know," Blaster says, sounding like a warrior accustomed to such harsh truths. It's directly after that Blaster's taken into custody, and it's hard not to feel like this isn't fair either.

In the great tradition of using simple narrative set-ups to explore moral situations, Budiansky has managed to make us thoroughly sympathize with an Autobot deserter. So too are we made to see that blindly obeying the Autobot command structure − which is essential to so many Transformers stories − as something contemptible.

Sure, it's pulp sci-fi with cliffhangers and some very broad-stroke characterization. But what it's doing is actually rather radical. (Especially – if it need to said – for a kids' comic about alien robots.)

Budiansky was also writing the four-issue mini-series *Transformers: Headmasters* (#1-4, July 1987 – Jan 1988) at the time, and his schedule necessitated a fill-in. So — despite the promise of "Blaster's fate revealed!" at the end of issue #32 — issues #33-34 (Oct-Nov 1987) reprinted the first original British Transformers story, "Man of Iron." This left the dramatic cliffhanger unresolved for an extra two months, and given how dramatic that cliffhanger is, it's hard not to imagine that figuring out how to resolve it might have played into the delay.

You might think that, after issue #32, Blaster would reconnect with the Throttlebots. But that never happens – at least not on-panel. When the story picks up again in issue #35 (Dec 1987), it remains focused on Blaster, and this continues into issue #36 (Jan 1988), which is effectively the culmination of the storyline. Goldbug and the other Throttlebots would return in issue #37 (Feb 1988), which is a kind of denouement to the storyline that also sets up the one that follows.

Issue #35 – by Budiansky, Perlin, Akin, and Garvey – is entitled "Child's Play," and it opens with a splash page of a kid being shot. Or so it seems. At the time, kids with toy guns being shot by police was a major news story, and legislation was passed to require that toy guns had a bright strip of color on them to help policemen identify them as toys. Of course, the image is all the more dramatic because it has nothing to do with Blaster — and is thus more surprising.

The child is actually faking. He's part of a group of four who's playing, with no adult supervision, on a section of railroad tracks. Sadly, the boy who's symbolically killed is the only Black child of the bunch, perpetuating the old cliché of the Black teammate dying (implicitly because he's more expendable). In addition to the Black boy, there's a White girl, who spends most of her time insecurely gripping her teddy bear. The other two kids are White boys. But at least an attempt is made to make the group of four children more diverse (an attempt not out of line with the inclusion of Asian character Charlie Fong, in issues #29-30).

The Protectobots soon arrive with the captive Blaster, and they contact Grimlock. Grimlock, who's only been shown on a single page since Blaster and Goldbug defected, is again seen here, and he's just as arrogant as before. Here, the story increases his negative depiction and answers the question about how the rest of the Autobots feel about him. After Grimlock pushes Wheeljack aside in order to rant about Blaster, Wheeljack thinks:

> Seems the only thing out simple-circuited commander's interested in is *getting even*, not stopping our enemies, the *Decepticons!*
>
> Can't hardly blame Blaster for going his own way… maybe I should *help* him…

It's a little heavy-handed, like most comics of the time, but it works. Implicitly, the other Autobots aren't so dumb as to think Grimlock's a fine leader, but their loyalty to the Autobot command structure is so great that they don't take action. Blaster and Goldbug may have defected, rather than return to face Grimlock's wrath for something they didn't do wrong. But no Autobot at the Ark has defied Grimlock in a way that might coalesce the others into open rebellion.

In this sequence, Grimlock also mentions that the Ark has been repaired, and we see it being refueled in preparation for take-off. This development is handled rather quickly, but it's a major one. In the early days of the comic, the fact that the Ark was buried and incapable of flying was important to the premise of the series, since it effectively stranded the Transformers on Earth. Now, it seems that all the Ark needed was a leader who made its repairs a priority.

Since Grimlock hasn't been shown often, we may assume this has been his focus – and that this focus contrasts with that of Optimus Prime, who was more concerned with other things, such as fighting Decepticons and saving threatened humans. And although we haven't seen much of the Decepticons either, it's not as if they haven't been up to anything. Indeed, we may see Buster Witwicky's starring role in issue #31 as an illustration of Grimlock's lack of concern, when it comes to the Decepticons. Had Optimus Prime still been alive, that could have been a more conventional Transformers tale, with Autobots versus Decepticons. Instead, the Autobots were absent, yielding the starring role to Buster.

Later in the story, we get another, slightly shorter sequence with Grimlock, in which he's shown overseeing the construction of a chair designed to torture Blaster, upon his return to the Ark. It's another way this story ups the ante, in preparation for Grimlock's larger role in the following issue. When Grimlock hears that Blaster's position isn't moving, he orders the Ark to prepare for takeoff.

Returning to the present issue, the Protectobots spot signs of the Combaticons, so they stow Blaster, in his tape deck mode and with a lock on him that prevents him from transforming, in a pipe. The Protectobots soon find the Combaticons, who combine into their gestalt form, Bruticus. The Protectobots follow suit, combining to form Defensor. This smacks of an editorial dictum to feature these combined forms, which was a major (and popular) feature of these toys – and which wasn't seen when the two teams fought in issue #32. Their rematch here, despite featuring these combined forms and being granted more space, feels rather like a a retread of the previous battle – right down to Blaster's timely intervention, which we'll get to in a moment. The one stand-out element of the fight is when the giant robots pick up abandoned trains from the nearby tracks and swing them at one another – a dramatic image also chosen for the cover (although the effect of that image, on the cover, is severely lessened by the coloring; Bruticus and Defensor are each depicted as a single color).

More satisfying is the emphasis on Blaster, since he's the focus of the larger storyline, and on the kids. Budiansky often excelled at these human stories, and the entire storyline can be read as a series of episodes in which various humans encounter the Transformers: Charlie Fong (in issues #29-30), Buster Witwicky and his girlfriend (in issue #31), Big Steve (in issue #32), and now these kids. While none of these humans stick around too long, the strategy of using them helps to ground stories about alien robots in recognizable human characters.

The kids find Blaster in the pipe and remove the lock on him, allowing him to transform. Almost immediately, a high-tension tower collapses, due to the fight between Defensor and Bruticus, and Blaster has to dive to shield the kids from it. Budiansky, who's characterized Blaster as a tough-minded warrior who saved Big

Steve despite that human's actions, continues Blaster's characterization here. After he's saved the kids, fulfilling his promise to protect them if they agree to listen to them, Blaster *gripes* about how he's had to save them: "Pretty lousy one-sided deal I made with you, huh?" It's a small touch – Blaster still does what's right, and it's only a single line of dialogue. But it's something that it's hard to imagine most of the Autobots uttering – and it does wonders for making Blaster distinct and interesting as a character (which is important, since he's the focus of this storyline).

Bruticus apparently defeats Defensor, then turns to Blaster. Knowing he's outmatched, Blaster claims that he was the Protectobots' prisoner and has "no loyalty for them or any of the Autobots!" It's a clever little twist, because it demonstrates Blaster's military thinking and his willingness to take strategies (like this one) that the other Autobots probably wouldn't. But it also plays into the continuing themes of loyalty and treason. Of course, we know that Blaster's still loyal to the Autobots' *values*, even if he's not loyal to the Autobots' *government*.

Grimlock doesn't understand this distinction. Interestingly, Bruticus *does*. He orders Blaster to prove his defection by killing one of the human children. This, too, is a cliché; we've all seen far too many movies in which the bad guys make such a demand, as if just because someone's a villain should mean they have no compunction against killing civilians. This cliché makes a bit more sense here, where it's less akin to killing a civilian and more akin to killing an animal – given that the Transformers are of another (probably superior) species. But there's no reason for Bruticus to think that disloyalty to the Autobots should require such a complete and total abandonment of Blaster's previous values. Bruticus is probably only entertaining himself by seeing Blaster struggle with the conundrum, but it's quite a conundrum.

Essentially, Blaster has to choose between killing a human child and being killed himself. All along, Budiansky's characterized Blaster as a warrior, capable of tough choices, but he's also characterized Blaster as valuing human life. This entire storyline revolves around Blaster's decision to desert the other Autobots – another tough decision. Now, Blaster is being morally tested – an apt situation for a deserter who's the protagonist of a moral story. If we take Bruticus at his word (a questionable assumption), logic would seem to dictate that Blaster kill the kid, since someone's going to die anyway and Blaster's far more capable of waging war against the Decepticons. But of course, this *feels* wrong to us, since a terrorist threat feels like no excuse for executing an innocent child. Essentially, Blaster's being put into a situation in which he has to decide whether he's ultimately the tough-minded warrior Budiansky has characterized him as being or whether he's a human-loving Autobot, with moral values we'd recognize.

With Bruticus's gun to him, Blaster raises *his* gun at the kids. The story really sells the point, and not only through Blaster's earlier grumbling about how protecting them is a "lousy one-sided deal." "I've got to go through with this or *I'm* dead!" he thinks, and we're all familiar with how thought balloons grant a view into a character's interior space. He says what he thinks Bruticus wants to hear, about using these "little runts" as "target practice."

Sammy – the Black boy seen "dying" on the first page – bravely steps forward. These kids have only known Blaster for a few minutes, so it's not surprising that they'd believe Blaster would kill one of them, especially since he's *saying* that he will.

And then Blaster fires. And Sammy falls.

Blaster apparently executes a kid, in *Transformers* #35 (Dec 1987).

That first page now appears to be a bit of foreshadowing, underlining the horror of Sammy's actual death at Blaster's hands, later in the story.

As Sammy's friends mourn him, Bruticus complements Blaster for being so *"brave."* And while Bruticus is distracted, Blaster conveniently makes short work of Bruticus by toppling an electrical tower into the Decepticon.

And then Sammy sits up. It was all an act. That first page wasn't foreshadowing of Sammy's actual death; it was an indicator of how good Sammy is at faking his own death in toy-gun fights – a skill he later uses when it really counts.

Later, after the Protectobots have revived, Blaster prepares to surrender himself again, provided the children are allowed to leave safely. It's a little odd that Blaster didn't try to sneak off before the Protectobots recovered, but this allows for the story's twist endings. Blaster explains that helping humans was what first got him into hot water with Grimlock (back in issue #28). In the first twist ending, Hotspot decides to let Blaster go. It's essentially the reverse of issue #32's ending, where the twist was Hotspot turning on Blaster. The Protectobots watch as Blaster takes off with the kids in Blast Off, one of the Combaticons whose alternate form is a space shuttle – to which is now affixed the mode-lock device, previously used on Blaster.

There's no reason for Blaster to escape in this way, except to fulfill the kids' dream of going into space. Outer space is obviously an essential element to the Transformers stories, and it's also something that fascinates children. That childhood joy is on full display here, as the kids get to experience weightlessness, and this comes off very successfully. But then comes the final twist: through a window, the kids spot a craft in pursuit, firing at them.

It's the Ark, having been restored, after 34 issues, to space-worthy status. Grimlock's taking things into his own hands, and the final conflict with Blaster – in which Grimlock has by far the superior forces – can't be long off.

Issue #36 (Jan 1988) doesn't only mark the conclusion (such as it is) of the Blaster saga. It also marked the one-year anniversary of the death of Optimus Prime – a year that had (perhaps surprisingly, given Optimus Prime's central role in the series) been tremendously successful, creatively, for the title. It was also the first issue penciled by José Delbo, who would become the title's regular penciler. Budiansky remained as writer, while Akin and Garvey remained as inkers through the next issue.

One of the hallmarks of Budiansky's run on the title was odd, often delightful jumps between issues. While this would sometimes drop a set of characters or a plotline, these sorts of dislocations could also be fascinating, generating a sense in readers that they had no idea what to expect next, nor even who would star in the next story. This kind of dislocation is on display in issue #36, which begins "several hours, Earth time, before the end of last issue's story" and focuses on Sky Lynx, a previously unseen Autobot who transformed into a space shuttle. Flashbacks show us that Wheeljack called Cybertron to summon Sky Lynx. As Sky Lynx approaches Earth, he sees the Ark taking off.

In the previous issue, we saw that Wheeljack was questioning Grimlock's leadership. It now appears that he took action – by calling Sky Lynx. He might not have deserted, but he's the first of the other Autobots to make a *choice* and to disobey the Autobot leader.

That leader's character doesn't improve here. On the first page featuring Grimlock, he *strangles* Wheeljack, simply for not finding Blaster's ship fast enough.

On Blast Off, the Decepticon space shuttle piloted by Blaster, we again see the kids from the previous issue playing and celebrating their weightlessness – essentially an extended scene from the previous issue. We then catch up to that issue's ending, replaying it.

On the one hand, this leap backwards in time is a way of inserting Sky Lynx retroactively into the story. On the other, it's a pretty sophisticated technique for a comic that's too often dismissed as a toy catalog in panel form.

Blast Off can't outrun the Ark, and Blaster can't risk injuring the children, so Blaster intends to surrender. But Sammy, eager to repay Blaster for helping him and the other three kids, takes it upon himself to throw Blaster through an airlock. When the Ark swallows up the Decepticon, Wheeljack and the others – who were surprised to find Blaster apparently working with the Decepticon Blast Off – are surprised to discover that only four human children are inside.

There are a few errors in this sequence. It's not clear how Sammy and the other kids didn't suffer from decompression, when he throws Blaster from the ship. Then, as Blaster goes sailing out into space, the artists make the mistake of illustrating Blaster arcing away from *Sky Lynx*, not from Blast Off. It's an easy mistake, when dealing with toys, especially when both are space shuttles.

Blast Off, in space shuttle mode, is depicted as absurdly small, relative to those around him. From *Transformers* #36 (Jan 1988).

Then, when the Autobots have Blast Off inside the Ark, the Decepticon space shuttle is depicted as about the size of a regular Transformer in robot mode — despite that the Decepticon's space shuttle form is clearly supposed to be much bigger. These kinds of errors of size were incredibly common, and they're a side effect of the fact that the toys didn't retain any consistent scale. For example, Blaster, Soundwave, and the cassette tapes were obviously very small in their alternate forms, yet were usually drawn much larger (and to scale with one another) in robot mode. Blast Off represents an example of the opposite problem, in which a Transformer's alternate form was very *large*. When he's on the Ark, he's drawn about the size of his toy, but a space shuttle is an order of magnitude larger — and larger than the other Combaticons' vehicle modes. Transformers are clearly able to inhabit Blast Off, when he's in the form of a space shuttle. (This is shown in a key scene in *Transformers: The Movie*, but it's implicit in this comic too, given that the humans float inside the space shuttle as if it's a normal space shuttle in size.) If we took Blast Off's small size, when in the Ark, literally, the children would have somehow shrunk. Scale would remain a problem for Transformers stories, although it's generally become less egregious in recent years. (Michael Bay, in particular, was keen to keep the scale constant, and although his Transformers movies do change characters' scales, they do so to a lesser extent and avoid making it as obvious a problem as it is in this issue of the comic.)

Adrift in space, Blaster thinks about how humans are "more trouble than they're worth!" – another instance of his characterization as a warrior with a less than rosy view of his own humanitarian values. Blaster's luckily – though rather improbably – able to steer himself toward a communication satellite and commandeer it, using its "stabilizing rockets" to steer it. Amusingly, we see a family in New Jersey lose their television signal, unaware that this is the consequence of living alien machines battling in orbit.

Back on the Ark, we're treated to Wheeljack escorting the kids around. We haven't seen the sprawling, alien interior of the Ark like this since the early issues, and it's nice to see it again, especially through these children's eyes. There's also a nice bit of humor, when Wheeljack uses a machine to outfit the children with spacesuits, then indulges Daisy – the female child – but outfitting her teddy bear in a spacesuit too. A teddy bear in a spacesuit is a neat idea, and the charm of it helps to make up for some of the issue's deficits.

This prosaic sequence is cut short, however, when the children are summoned to Grimlock. Wheeljack is clearly concerned, although he doesn't let on, for the children's benefit. Grimlock is just as block-headed, or even evil, as we would expect him to be. Seated on an elaborate, technological throne, he says scornfully that the children aren't just humans but "not even *full-size* humans! They no deserve court trail!" When the children refuse to give

Grimlock information about Blaster's location, the tyrannical Autobot leader sentences the children to death for helping a traitor and orders the sentence to "be carried out *immediately!*" Wheeljack stands silent, and the other Autobots look aghast.

But Grimlock's not as dumb as he may seem. He quickly reveals to one of his Dinobot comrades that he has no intention of killing the children but knows Blaster will try to save them.

It's all very dramatically done, but just as dramatic is what follows: Grimlock, sword in hand, forces the frightened children to *walk the plank*. In space. Although hardly unique, it's another cool visual idea – one used on the issue's cover.

Before Blaster can arrive on his communications satellite, however, Sky Lynx rescues the kids – having been radioed to do so by Wheeljack. For his part, Blaster makes it to the back of the Ark, where he lands… only apparently to be incinerated by the Ark's rockets, as Grimlock's apparently ordered the ship to pursue Sky Lynx.

Sky Lynx flies into "a meteor shower" – which is depicted more like how sci-fi wrongly depicts asteroid belts as densely packed. With the Ark unable to pursue, Grimlock leads the Dinobots after Sky Lynx, who leaps from "meteor" to "meteor" until the Dinobots surround him. Again, Grimlock's not as dumb as he seems: he knows the children have a limited air supply, and he's trying to force Blaster's hand.

On board the Ark, Blaster, having survived the ship's thrusters, climbs inside. The other Autobots are only too eager to abandon Grimlock and follow Blaster instead. It may seem as if they've been reading Blaster's exploits the same way we have, but it's a demonstration of how authoritarian the Autobots can be. Dissatisfaction with Grimlock is obviously at profound levels, but the Autobots apparently need another candidate for a leader to rally behind before they can take action.

But like a good Autobot leader, Blaster's more focused on the danger to the children. He wants to solve *that* before discussing leadership. And when he sees that Grimlock's got the children and Sky Lynx surrounded, Blaster dismisses any attack upon the Dinobots as too dangerous for the humans. Instead, he insists upon surrendering – the only way he knows "to guarantee their safety."

And that's, really, how the Blaster saga ends. With another twist, another cliffhanger.

Blaster surrenders, effectively ending his saga, on the final page of *Transformers* #36 (Jan 1988).

Before addressing issue #37, it's worth mentioning that the previous two issues had a denouement of sorts that was exclusive to the British Transformers comic. Actually, the British comic ran several new stories between the U.S. issues that comprised the Blaster storyline, but those new British tales had their own plots and didn't connect to the Blaster / Goldbug one. However, the reprint of American issues #35-36 was followed by a single-issue story, in U.K. issue #125 (26 Dec 1987) that *did* connect to the American stories.

It so happened that this was that year's Christmas issue, and the British series (like many British comics at the time) had a tradition of Christmas stories. This one – scripted by Ian Rimmer from a plot by Simon Furman, penciled by Jeff Anderson, and inked by Stephen Baskerville – focused on Starscream. In the American series, Starscream was offline at the time, but in the British series he had recently been revived. In the story, he pines for Cybertron, his revival having given him a new perspective on his petty desire for killing Autobots and gaining Decepticon leadership. That itself may be seen as an interesting commentary, intended or not, on

Grimlock's petty dictatorship. To his annoyance, Starscream meets a human and uncharacteristically agrees to fly him around, so that the human can show him the meaning of Christmas. When the human orders Starscream to land and help a bus of elderly humans who are stuck in a snowbank, an Autobot interferes, naturally assuming Starscream is a threat.

It's here that the story intersects with the Blaster saga, because that Autobot is Streetwise, a Protectobot. Streetwise and Starscream fight for a couple pages, endangering the bus. Their battle is stopped by the human, who chastises Streetwise for making assumptions that endangered people. Starscream, who previously seemed confused as to why anyone would help the humans in the bus, now frees them from the snowdrift – apparently just to spite Streetwise. Streetwise lets Starscream go and escorts the bus, while Starscream hangs out with his human companion… before finally conceding and saying "Merry Christmas" before he leaves.

It's not a great story by any means, but as a denouement to the Blaster saga, it does reflect some of the themes of that saga – and not only through Starscream looking beyond the desire for leadership. That Streetwise is able to look beyond the Autobot-Decepticon conflict underlines how that conflict's really secondary to the Blaster storyline, in which the main conflict is between Autobots and about Autobot values. Despite his status as a Protectobot, Streetwise's great failing in the story is his failure to protect the humans on the bus – and this reflects the Autobots' lack of concern for humans under Grimlock's rule.

But there's also another implication of the story. If it's taken in the sequence in which it was published – which makes sense – it suggests that the Protectobots never returned to the Ark, after they let Blaster go. Essentially, they *defected too*. If we think of Blaster and Goldbug's defection as a meme, it's apparently infectious.

To some degree, it makes sense that the Protectobots didn't return. They would presumably have spread the word of what they learned from Blaster about his innocence, and there's no sign of this having happened in the American stories. On the other hand, it's odd that Grimlock, who's so concerned about defection, wouldn't notice that the Protectobots had also gone AWOL – although perhaps he's too obsessed with Blaster to even notice the Protectobots' absence. That certainly wouldn't be out of character with Grimlock's depiction in the American stories, even if it's odd that the Protectobots disappear from them, despite co-starring in two issues.

The following American issue – #37 (Feb 1988), also by Budiansky, Delbo, Akin, and Garvey – follows up on the Throttlebots plot. It also features Ratbat and the Earth-bound Decepticons, who haven't been seen for a few issues (outside of the Combaticons). The story focuses on another human character, a government agent named Barnett who's been put in charge of the Throttlebots. (As with Charlie Fong, there's a nice bit of diversity at work here, because Barnett is black.) He comes to believe in the distinction between the Autobots and the Decepticons, but it's a distinction lost on his superiors. After another Decepticon attack, the government publicly orders the destruction of the six robots it has in custody. To the horror of many child readers, we watch as the six Throttlebots are crushed and turned into cubes, with Goldbug (which whom we most identify) crushed last for dramatic effect.

But of course there's a twist: Barnett removed the Autobots' "brain modules" and connected them to six of his son's battery-powered toy cars. It's a cool twist, in part because of the Transformers' existence as a toy line.

With Barnett at a loss, the Throttlebots suggest visiting Buster Witwicky. The Autobots' plan is to return to the Ark, which they don't know has been repaired and left the Earth, and they believe that Buster is the only human who would be allowed to approach it. Buster leaves with Barnett.

But Ratbat and the Predacons, having already attacked the R.A.A.T. base and found the Throttlebots absent, find the Witwicky auto repair business. Ratbat menaces Buster's dad – a character who made his debut in the very first issue (Sept 1984). After a cut between panels, we see Ratbat do something that causes debris to fly out of the Witwicky garage, implying that he may have killed Buster's dad.

When Buster and Barnett stop at a mall for batteries for the toy cars, Ratbat and the Predacons arrive. The idea of putting the Throttlebots into toy cars thus allows for a fun chase sequence, as they flee through the mall from the Decepticons. Extreme points of view, necessary to put the toy cars large and in the foreground, enhance the sequence. Buster and Ratbat, having battled in issue #31, get a rematch here, ending in a victory for Buster when Barnett sends one of the steel doors common in shopping malls crashing down onto Ratbat's head, pinning him. Batnett stays with the other Throttlebots, while Buster flees to the Ark with the toy inhabited by Goldbug's consciousness.

Of course, the Ark is gone. But the Autobots have left behind some equipment, including a transceiver capable of radioing Cybertron for help. With Buster's help, Goldbug's able to send out an S.O.S.

But Ratbat has apparently escaped the mall, after we last left him. Somehow, he's stowed away in Buster's tape player – from which he earlier retrieved batteries to save Goldbug's toy form, when it ran out of energy. Ratbat enters the Ark, and in the final two panels of the story, picks up Goldbug's toy form and crushes it, while menacing a scared Buster.

It's an excellent cliffhanger in a series that excelled at them. Goldbug seems dead. Buster is at Ratbat's mercy. Buster's father may be dead. The fate of Barnett and the other Throttlebots remains unknown. Meanwhile, the Autobots are in space, apparently still under the control of Grimlock, to whom Blaster has surrendered. In other words, all seems lost.

Normally, one might expect that this would be followed by a return to space and to the Blaster plot. But the Headmasters mini-series had concluded, and its characters needed to be added to the main title. It's unclear whether this was a result of editorial fiat or not; Budiansky seems to have enjoyed writing the Headmasters, if the quality of that mini-series is any indication, and he may not have wanted to directly continue the Blaster cliffhanger. In the final issue of the Headmasters mini-series (#4, Jan 1988), the Autobot Headmasters receive an S.O.S. from Earth. It's the same signal sent in this issue.

So instead of the main title returning to the Blaster plot, the

Headmasters arrive in issue #38 (Mar 1988), in which the Headmasters basically take over the title. The issue reveals that Buster Witwicky's father survived and introduces Buster's brother, Spike Witwicky. In that issue, the former home of the Ark is trashed, and Galen – who formed the head of Fortress Maximus, leader of the Autobot Headmasters – dies. Spike takes Galen's place. (Essentially, Spike and Buster were the same character, but the comic used the name Buster and the cartoon the name Spike. The sudden introduction of Spike in the comic was almost certainly done to comply with the specs of the toy, which listed Spike Witwicky instead of Galen.)

Issue #39 (Apr 1988) reveals Buster's fate; Ratbat took him prisoner at the end of issue #37. Barnett and the Throttlebots also return. The main arc of the issue belongs to Spike, who's adjusting to essentially being in charge of the Autobot Headmasters. Still, despite much of the important action taking place in Earth orbit (where the Autobot Headmasters' ship is located), there's no word from the Ark.

Issue #40 (May 1988) sees Goldbug getting his body rebuilt, introduces the Pretenders (robots within organic shells), and follows up on Optimus Prime death in issue #24. That issue ended with a characteristic Budiansky twist by revealing that Optimus Prime survived, his personality recorded on a computer disc. He doesn't get a new body in issue #40, but the Autobot Headmasters discover his continued existence as a disembodied computer program.

It's not until issue #41 (June 1988) that the Ark (including Blaster and Grimlock) is seen again. Even then, we essentially see them from the point of view of the Autobot Headmasters, who finally notice the Ark's presence nearby. Grimlock, who's still ruling the Autobots like a self-obsessed tyrannical king (complete with crown), doesn't take kindly to the news that Spike Witwicky, a human, is in charge of these other Autobots. Nor does he like that they're harboring Goldbug, whom Grimlock regards as a traitor. When we finally see Blaster, he's on that torture seat seen in issue #35. Blaster's not shown screaming, but the seat seems to hold him in a permanent stress position, as well as electrocuting him when his captors will it. All the Autobots of both camps assemble on the

Moon, letting us see many characters who hadn't been seen for some time. Because Fortress Maximus is injured, Blaster substitutes for him in a fight with Grimlock, with the winner to become Autobot leader. So we finally get to see the two fight one another – which perhaps ought to have been the conclusion of the Blaster storyline – even if this story is submerged within a tale that's really about the Headmasters. If the scene on the Moon didn't feature enough Transformers, the Decepticons arrive, seizing the opportunity to rescue their captured comrades. In the resulting chaos, Blaster and Grimlock actually give up their feud and chase off the Decepticons. But the Ark's damaged, incapable of flight, and energy's running low.

To make matters worse, Steelhaven, the Autobot Headmasters' ship, has left during the conflict, under the orders of Fortress Maximus, who himself has remained on the Moon. In the end, Fortress Maximus explains that he's ordered Goldbug to take the ship to Nebulos, the planet that was the setting of the Headmasters mini-series, in order to construct a new body for Optimus Prime. And that's just what happens in the next issue (#42, July 1988). Not coincidentally, a new Optimus Prime toy had come out, as part of the Powermaster sub-line, in which humanoids transformed not into robot heads or guns but into engines.

Issue #43 (Aug 1988) was another fill-in, adapting an episode of the cartoon that didn't fit into the comic's continuity. Issue #44 (Sept 1988) finally reconnected with Sky Lynx and the children whom Blaster took into space — whose parents (who sadly are never seen) must have assumed them to be dead after all this time. Sky Lynx is shown returning the children to early in issue #45 (Oct 1988).

You'd think, after all this tumult, that we'd be shown Optimus Prime returning to the Moon and uniting the various Autobot factions under him. Yet that happens *between issues*. Instead, the series focused on increasingly silly stories, and it's widely acknowledged that the series declined in quality, if not went off the proverbial rails, during this period. The Headmasters were the beginning of a series of gimmicky toys – like the Targetmasters, Powermasters, and Pretenders – that seemed to overtake the series. Before long, Optimus Prime was operating on Earth, and the conflict between Grimlock, Blaster, and Fortress Maximus was essentially forgotten in favor of new – and less successful – stories.

During the extended Blaster storyline, Budiansky had managed fairly masterfully to introduce new characters, weaving them into the continuing story in ways that often solved narrative problems, rather than distracting too much from the main story. He managed to keep the plates spinning from issues #28-37 (although issues #33-34 were fill-ins) – the title's only single, coherent story that could rival that of issues #5-12 (June 1985 - Jan 1986), which focused on the Autobots' slow recovery after their total defeat in issue #4 (Mar 1985). In this comparison, the Blaster storyline had the advantage of being a lot more artistically consistent – thanks to Don Perlin, Ian Akin, and Brian Garvey. But with issue #38, the title went in a very different direction, only reconnecting with the Blaster storyline's plot threads in #41 and #44. By the time the title had established a new status quo, with Optimus Prime back in charge of the Autobots, the kind of narrative dislocations that had served so successfully in earlier issues seemed to have taken over and alienated many regular readers, who couldn't count on plots being adequately followed through and who often didn't know which characters were where at any given time. Surely, some of this wasn't Budiansky's fault, but rather a side effect of the constant introduction of whole lines of new Transformers, who needed explanations for how they came to exist as well as something to do. But the Blaster storyline was in many ways the end of a simpler era for the comic.

The return of Optimus Prime also underlined the authoritarian nature of the Autobots. Sure, Optimus Prime was a great leader and a great character. But Blaster had been characterized well, and issue #36 seemed to set up the possibility that all of his trials were logically leading him to (literally) dethrone Grimlock – whose rule could then be regarded as a temporary one, while the Autobots figured out how to go on without Optimus Prime.

Even in this, the Autobots seemed especially helpless without a leader to fall behind. No one but Blaster – and to a lesser extent, Wheeljack and Goldbug – dared to challenge Grimlock's commands, even though they *knew* he was in the wrong. The Autobots have pretty consistently been depicted as an authoritarian bunch, and they're perfectly willing – in the absence of a rival for the throne – to continue executing the orders of a megalomaniac tyrant. They only dare rally behind Blaster when he's in front of them and Grimlock's away. And when Grimlock returns with Blaster as a captive, the Autobots apparently fall right back to executing Grimlock's orders.

"What can be done?" goes the thinking. "He's our leader."

Of course, all that's necessary for the rise of a tyrant is for people who know better to do nothing. The Blaster storyline is a perfect illustration of this, but it's also an exploration of the Autobots' authoritarian impulses.

In this sense, Optimus Prime's solution is no solution at all. Sure, he's a good leader, and it's easy as a Transformers fan to see him as the *rightful* leader, since we like him and he was the first Autobot leader. But a benevolent dictator, even one as good as Optimus Prime, isn't a solution to the lack of any recognizable political instinct in the Autobot ranks. Essentially, the Autobots are sheep – perhaps even programmed to *be* sheep. And after Optimus Prime's return, we can't pretend this isn't so. Even Grimlock and Blaster are only too glad to defer to the returned and rightful king. What the Autobots need is a good political education. And for all of Optimus Prime's goodness, this is the one thing he never provides.

The arrival of the Headmasters might have sidetracked the Blaster storyline. But Optimus Prime's return did so in a deeper, spiritual way, forcing all of the issues invoked by the storyline to be swept under the rug. Is it any surprise that Optimus Prime often seemed tired and listless, for the remainder of the series?

If the Blaster storyline is an interrogation of power – and of the Autobots' authoritarian impulses – the genie can't go back in the bottle. Grimlock's not the problem. The Autobots' political nature is.

That nature isn't something invented by this story. But this story is the fullest exploration of it.

It's a message that's all too vital, as we consider threats to democracy and witness nations – sometimes even our own – cater to authoritarian impulses. The idea of crimes against humanity, articulated at Nuremberg, is predicated upon the ethical stance that soldiers cannot legally obey an illegal order – it's up to each soldier to disobey, consequences be damned, and each soldier is legally liable for their actions, even when they follow orders. Blaster and Goldbug had the courage to say "no."

And that's a vital, noble message – which, not coincidentally, also happened to produce many of the best issues in Transformers history.[*]

---

[*] First serialized on Sequart Organization's website in June 2014.

Transformers: Headmasters
and Cycles of Violence

When the Headmasters toys debuted, Marvel's Transformers comic was selling well, in part due to the excitement surrounding 1986's *Transformers: The Movie*. And so the Headmasters got to debut not in the monthly Transformers comic but in their own four-issue, bimonthly mini-series, titled *Transformers: Headmasters* (#1-4, July 1987 - Jan 1988). It was written by regular series writer Bob Budiansky, penciled by Frank Springer (who'd illustrated several Transformers stories), and inked by regular series inkers Ian Akin and Brian Garvey.

Usually, new characters were introduced either by their being built on Earth or their coming to Earth from Cybertron. *Headmasters* took a very different route by avoiding Earth altogether, in the process telling what amounted to an alternate version of the Transformers' arrival on Earth, except set on the planet Nebulos.

It's a fascinating idea, really. When the Transformers began, their time on Cybertron before their departure was glossed over relatively quickly. The needs of the story demanded this, because there was an awful lot to explain, including the very *concept* of alien robots that transformed into vehicles. The idea that these robots were engaged in a civil war also had to be dramatized, as did how they acquired their forms resembling Earth vehicles, not to mention their adjustment to organic life that *drove* these vehicles rather than *being* the vehicles. That's an awful lot to do and still have the requisite action set on Earth.

Headmasters was freed from much of this. Knowing Cybertron was successful with readers, the story could dwell there a bit more. The first issue's opening splash page began with Decepticon leader Scorponok torturing captured Autobot slaves. The following Autobot-Decepticon battle is depicted as a scene of carnage, and Budiansky's captions emphasize the dead and the wounded, as if he's describing a battlefield of the American Civil War, rather than sci-fi robots duking it out.

Freed from the need to follow the existing story for how Optimus Prime and Megatron wound up on Earth, Budiansky imagined another reason: that Autobot leader Fortress Maximus was tired of war without end and saw no alternative. While his soldiers celebrate, Fortress Maximus broods and angrily corrects them. Optimus Prime took the Ark away from Cybertron to stop a meteor shower, was attacked by Decepticons, and inadvertently crashed on Earth. But Fortress Maximus *targeted* Nebulos as a planet where they could start a new life, freed from almost half a million years of war that he felt had gotten him and his comrades nothing.

Unlike Optimus Prime upon arriving on Earth, Fortress Maximus isn't ignorant about organic life. On the contrary, he quite logically intends to contact the planet's leaders.

Finally, freed from needing to adhere to Earth, *Headmasters* was free to imagine its own planet. Nebulos is a sci-fi utopia, straight out of planetary romance stories — right down to the skin-tight sci-fi clothing. One of the Autobots, while landing, calls it a paradise. We soon learn this isn't entirely right — there's certainly political strife on the planet. But it's a beautiful place that's a peace.

You knew the Transformers weren't going to change Earth too radically, but all bets were off when it came to Nebulos.

In a sequence recalling the Frankenstein monster inadvertently drowning a little girl, the Autobot Chromedome stumbled upon a couple making out. Gort, the male of the couple, tries to defend the female, but he stumbles and falls into a ravine, hitting his head. The injury looks severe, and the female is upset. Chromedome stutters, "My apologies, carbon-based life form." He adds, "I... I hope you companion can be... repaired..." The sequence might be slightly heavy-handed, but it's a classic illustration of a cultural misunderstanding. Chromedome's awkwardness, in encountering organic life, is the kind of stuff you expect more from good science fiction than Transformers stories.

The incident spurs a debate in the Council of Peers, the planet's governing body. The debate seems led by Lord Zarak, who argues for preemptive action, and Galen, who argues for restraint. But after another incident, caused by one of Zarak's men, the planet — which has experienced 10,000 years of peace — prepares for war.

In a marvelously theatrical sequence, Galen goes to open the planet's armory, aware that his "life is no longer his to control." While we could nitpick and say that it's unlikely such an armory would survive 10,000 years, the image is a powerful symbol for the savagery innate in the human condition. On Nebulos, this has been buried beneath a civilized, even utopian veneer. But it's still there, waiting to be unlocked and released.

Nebulos soon mounts an assault on the Autobots, and it's rich with poetic resonance. War has come to Nebulos, and there's no mistaking the savagery of what we're seeing. Many of the Autobots want to fight back — they're soldiers, after all — but Fortress Maximus forbids it. He came to Nebulos to *escape* war, not to spread it.

One of the most basic aspects of the Transformers is embodied in the "their war, our world" slogan, from the 2007 movie. Essentially, this means that the war between the Autobots and Decepticons has come to Earth — which is uninvolved in the war but happens to become a beachhead in it. As the factions adopt different strategies, only the question is how the humans will react to this war, of unfathomable technology, on our shores. The stories that result might explore human nature or Transformer nature, and they might explore the politics or morality of either or both. But no one can pretend our world isn't always at war.

This isn't the case with Nebulos. It would be easy to see this as a case of upping the ante by portraying the "our world" part of the equation in the most prosaic light possible, in order to add to the drama. That's not wrong. But there's depth to the depiction in *Headmasters*, which is shot through with the agony of war and the inability of brave and moral people to stop it. Implicit in this depiction is that idea that the Transformers are a virus, that by coming to Nebulos, Fortress Maximus has infected it somehow. It's hard for me not to put myself in Fortress Maximus's position and feel that everything I touch is contaminated.

The cover to *Transformers: Headmasters* #1 (July 1987).

There's a powerful sense of inevitability, that trait common to so much great literature, to this story. *Of course*, there would be misunderstandings between the aliens and the natives. *Of course*, some will be more trusting than others, and some will see the benefits to be gained from war. Nebulos was never going to remain the same, after the Transformers arrived. And *of course*, Fortress Maximus, who was brave enough to abandon his beloved Cybertron because he couldn't see an end to the cycle of violence, isn't going to accept that Nebulos has to descend so quickly into war.

And so Fortress Maximus leads a contingent of his Autobots to a native fortress, where he effectively surrenders. He and a few other prominent Autobots in his camp deactivate themselves in the most dramatic way possible: by removing their heads. Of course, this *particular* dramatic gesture isn't inevitable, but it's successful in shutting down Lord Zarak and his drive to war.

To its credit, this issue doesn't even feature the Decepticons arriving on Nebulos. It's entirely a sort of parable about war itself – and about the dramatic gestures that may be required, if one wishes to escape it.

As the story continues, we see Galen talking with Fortress Maximus's severed head, learning about the alien culture of the Transformers. This represents cultural relativism or the willingness to try to understand cultures different from one's own. Lord Zarak represents the opposite possibility, and he soon contacts the Decepticons on Cybertron. Scorponok is only too eager to represent the Autobots as the bad guys, and he soon comes to Nebulos and assaults its cities.

There's a certain poetry to Nebulos having *invited* the Decepticons. They don't simply *follow* the Autobots, as in the story of the Transformers' arrival on Earth. The Decepticons' arrival *isn't* inevitable. They're *summoned*.

It's in response to this that Galen perfects the Headmasters process. Unwilling to reactivate the decapitated Autobots but knowing that the Decepticons need to be stopped, Galen and his colleagues *become* the Autobots' heads, allowing him to control the technology necessary to stop the Decepticons.

When you consider that the idea behind the Headmasters stems from a pretty silly variation on the Transformers concept invented to sell toys, this is a pretty impressive origin story. It's quite remarkable for its cleverness.

Galen is successful in repelling the Decepticons. But part of the price he pays is alienating his girlfriend, the lovely Llyra, who's also Lord Zarak's daughter. The two clearly love one another, but Llyra loves Galen because he's a man of peace – unlike her father. Galen commanding Transformers in battle might please the people, but it spurs Llyra to say he's not the man she fell in love with.

And yes, she's absurdly beautiful (and like many Nebulans, scantily clad). But she's also a confident, thoughtful woman, capable of standing up to her father and to her lover.

If the rest of the series retained this level of quality, it would be a top-notch sci-fi story, as well as one of the best Transformers stories ever told. One of the most successful elements of the first two issues is that their stories feel so controlled. But the next two issues strain a bit under the weight of introducing new characters.

For example, issue #3 begins by introducing the previously unseen Terrorcons and Technobots, new teams of Decepticons and Autobots who combine to form Abominus and Computron, respectively. These characters weren't seen earlier, and their ability to combine into larger robots contradicts the comic's continuity, in which this feature first appeared on Earth. The sequence introduces these characters, but it has no effect on the plot.

The rest of issue #3 largely focuses on establishing the Decepticon Headmasters, commanded by Lord Zarak, who forms the head of Scorponok. The issue ends, much as *Transformers* #4 (Mar 1985) did: with the Decepticons' total victory. The Autobot Headmasters are defeated, Galen and his comrades are unconscious, and Llyra, having misunderstood the fight in which she was endangered, blaming Galen and not her father.

Issue #4 rushes through the creation of another class of Transformers: the Targetmasters. As with the Headmasters, the Autobot versions are created first, then the Decepticon versions. If the parallel to an arms race wasn't clear, in the case of the

Headmasters, it's certainly clear with the Targetmasters, which features Nebulans transforming into the Transformers' guns.

The final issue also, by necessity, has Galen and the other Nebulans who become the Autobot heads escape. Having received an S.O.S. from Earth (shown being sent in *Transformers* #37, Feb 1988), Galen prepares to depart, knowing the Decepticons will follow. Galen's now in the position that Fortress Maximus was, at the beginning of the mini-series: leaving the planet he loves. In Fortress Maximus's case, his departure was to escape the war that seemed to go inexorably with his planet. In Galen's case, his departure is to liberate his planet from war.

Fortress Maximus tried to escape the cycle of violence and failed. Galen can't escape it, but he might be able to take it with him, sparing the world he loves.

But the ending really belongs to Llyra. She's learned that her father was lying about Galen. She asks her lover for the truth, and we know she'll believe it. But Galen lies.

We may presume this is because he knows it wouldn't be safe for her to go with him, or that he loves her enough to want to spare her along with his planet. His own explanation, to his fellows, is less satisfying: he wouldn't be able to leave, knowing she still loved him, and he knows he has to leave for Nebulos's sake. This doesn't really make sense; of course, she loves him. But it's how Galen understands it, and their love is the final casualty of the war brought to Nebulos.

On the final page, we see the Autobots leaving for Earth – where they'd basically take over the monthly Transformers comic. In the final panel, we see Nebulos beginning to rebuild, while Llyra's shown crying. It's a little melodramatic, but it's a reminder that damage has been done to this planet. And there can be no pretending that this Transformers story ends happily, or with anything but a Pyrrhic victory for the good guys.

There's no doubt that *Headmasters* is pulpy stuff, and its final two issues aren't nearly as good as the first two. But it manages to weave an alternate version of the Transformers origin into a powerful parable for war – and the difficulty of escaping patterns of escalating force and violence, once they've begun. Partly because it was separate from the regular series, it's able to achieve an epic feeling. It's a good Transformers story, but it's also just good science fiction.[*]

---

[*] First published on Sequart Organization's website in June 2014.

Optimus Prime, Pedophile?

Did you know that the beloved leader of the Autobots once had a penchant for underage girls?

Or that a Megatron look-alike not only shared the same fetish, but repeatedly tried to *rape* those girls?

Or that contact between Transformers and underage girls was the point of an entire Transformers *line*?

All of this occurred in *official* Transformers products – a line that starred the original, Generation One versions of these characters.

To understand how this came about, we have to go back a little bit. In 2003, Takara – the Japanese company that releases Transformers toys in Japan and co-owns the franchise with Hasbro – launched a line of Transformers toys called Binaltech. These toys all transformed into cars – and only cars. The line had several distinguishing traits. Rather than being made-up cars, the car forms in the Binaltech line would be real-world models, lisenced from actual car manufacturers. (Volkswagon prevented a version of the character Bumblebee from transforming into a Beetle, not wanting – perhaps due to the company's World War II history – to be associated with "war toys.") Even cooler, the Binaltech cars would be reproduced in a consistent 1:24 scale,[1] correcting the annoying problem of inconsistent scale common to every other Transformers line. Moreover, the cars were cast primarily in metal, with rubber tires, and featured some pretty exacting detail – so much that Binaltech toys look like model cars, yet are still transform into robots. The car doors opened individually, and the front hoods lifted, revealing an engine block (which typically transformed into a gun for robot mode). To get all this to work, the transformations into robot mode were (for the time) notoriously difficult.

---

[1] 1:24 is about the scale of Hasbro's original M.A.S.K. line of toys, which ran from 1985 to 1988.

I recall seeing Binaltech toys, in the comic-book store I frequented the most often in Hawaii, which had Japanese import toys along a few of its walls. As someone who had Transformers toys as a child but who'd since stopped collecting toys entirely, I was instantly struck by how the Binaltech toys looked like how I'd always wanted Transformers toys to look. I resisted buying them; they were expensive. But they haunted me, and some months later, I surrendered to them − reigniting a love for toys that had laid dormant for years. My pocketbook has Binaltech to blame.

The toy line was conceived as consisting only of the Autobots, since they (usually) transformed into cars (and sold better, especially in Japan). But after the line proved successful, it was expanded to include a few Decepticons − who now also transformed, unlike most past incarnations, into real-life cars.

Attempts were made to expand the line into military vehicles. But keeping them at the same 1:24 scale, the toys would have been prohibitively large and expensive, especially for the time.

In the U.S., Hasbro released Binaltech toy molds under the Alternators name. To keep the price down, the metal used in Japan was swapped for cheap-looking plastic, which kind of defeated the line's whole point. Understandably, Alternators didn't sell well in the U.S., and several of the Japanese models were never released stateside. (On the other hand, a couple Alternators exclusives didn't see Japanese release − including a new car body for Ravage that was the only toy mold in the line to turn into into an animal, instead of a humanoid robot.)

In Japan, Binaltech had accompanying fiction. These Binaltech stories were officially set in the original Transformers universe, known as "Generation 1." The original Transformers animated series, originally set in the present day, jumped forward to 2005 for the 1986 film *Transformers: The Movie*. Whereas the American comics continued to be set in the present day, creating continuity problems, the irregularly-published Japanese comics were ostensibly set in the cartoon continuity and incorporated the movie's time jump. Whereas the third, post-movie cartoon season was set in 2006 in America, it was set in 2010 in Japan.[2] Since the Binaltech line was a return to G1-influenced Earth vehicles (after the diversions of *Beast Wars* and other lines), it made sense to tie the Binaltech stories to the G1 continuity. Thus, these stories were set between the movie and the cartoon's third season – which in Japan constituted a five-year gap.

In this material, a robot plague of sorts forced the Autobots to find new bodies, and the real-world car companies were eager to do their part for the cause of good. This explained the new figures, all of which had Generation 1 names. When a few Decepticons were added, the story explained that they had hijacked the Binaltech process. How they were going to get their old bodies back in time for the events of the third season (set in 2010, in Japanese continuity) was never explained.

In late 2005, as Binaltech was winding down, Takara launched a subline called Binaltech Asterisk. The subline featured repaints of existing Binaltech toys, along with PVC figurines of human girls who could be positioned to look like they were driving the toys in car mode. Although a bit scantily clad, the figures weren't over-the-top. The subline didn't do well and only saw three releases, none of which had an American equivalent.

In 2006, the Transformers toy line was in a transitional phase. The *Cybertron* cartoon and toy line was wrapping up, leaving a gap between it and the upcoming 2007 live-action movie. Both Hasbro and Takara were concerned with keeping *something* in stores until the movie, with its corresponding toys. In the states, Hasbro solved the problem with its Classics line, featuring newly redesigned versions of beloved original characters – along with toys that had been intended for the late Cybertron line.[3] Hasbro also added

---

[2] Yes, everything has to be as complicated as possible. In fact, whereas the American cartoon ended after a three-episode fourth season introducing the Headmasters, Japan rejected these episodes and continued the cartoon on its own. It would continue through three additional series (each one season, basically) and an original movie. Generation 1 continuity is in fact a branching monstrosity with several versions and multiple permutations of most of those versions.

[3] Although intended as a stopgap, the Classics line helped pave the way for subsequent redesigns of classic characters in the main line of Transformers toys.

Transformers to its multi-property Titanium Series, releasing die-cast Transformers toys for the first time since G1.

In Japan, Takara had its own, more ambitious plans for a Binaltech successor, called Kiss Players. Similar to Binaltech Asterisk, Kiss Players featured Binaltech toy molds, now recast in plastic instead of metal, with plastic figurines of scantily-clad girls. Some kind of accessory was also added – such as a surf board that turned into a sword. The line was helmed by toy designer and manga artist Yuki Ohshima, who had previously published a fan manga featuring the Transformers (including a crossover with Japan's version of the Go-Bots).

All of which sounds relatively benign. After all, past Transformers toys had included human figures. In fact, whole lines, going back to the Headmasters during Generation 1, incorporated humans (or extraterrestrial organic humanoids, depending on the continuity) as part of their gimmick. The Headmasters were humans in exosuits who transformed into the heads of the robot Transformers. The Targetmasters were humans who transformed into the robots' guns. The Powermasters were humans who transformed into the Transformers' engines, allowing them to transform and apparently acting as a power source.

Takara, which continued G1 continuity after its American cancellation, expanded these ideas with the Brainmasters – similar to the Headmasters, except that these diminutive human-sized partners would be pushed into the toy's chest, which then pushed the faceplate part of the Brainmaster up to form the robot face.[4] Takara also followed with the (perhaps unfortunately named) Breastmasters (part of the Breast Force) – smaller robots who, like some Transformers, had animal forms instead of humanoid ones (hence their being called Breast Animals). Like Targetmasters, these

---

[4] In American continuity, the Headmasters and their sentient Transformers partners were supposedly symbiotic, but in practice, one personality tended to control both – depending on which character was more dominant. In Japanese continuity, Headmasters were sentient and their larger robot partners were soulless "Transtectors." Brainmasters were the inverse, with a sentient Transformer's consciousness able to transfer into the smaller Brainmaster.

partners could transform into weapons for the larger robot; sort of like Powermasters, they could also form breastplate armor to "power up" the larger robot. While neither Brainmasters nor Breastmasters were human or organic, they continued the Headmaster / Targetmaster / Powermaster idea of a smaller partner "powering up" the larger Transformer.

Some time had passed between these and the Kiss Players line, but it had clear precedents — both in the scantily-clad females of Binaltech Asterisk and the tradition of Transformers having human "power up" partners. So what was the big deal about?

First, the Kiss Players girls looked like sexualized pre-teenagers, stylized in what many Americans consider "the manga look."[5] Although officially of age and said to be old enough to drive by the accompanying literature, Ohshima's artistic style deliberately exaggerated proportions to make the girls appear not only younger but actually underage.

That's problematic, but it's common to a lot of anime and manga. You can object to it, if you want, but it's nothing new.

But a more serious problem stemmed from the fact that the toy line needed a narrative justification for including these figurines. The largely continuity-free fiction for Binaltech Asterisk had simply told stories of humans and Transformers cooperating as part of an exchange program between Earth and Cybertron. But for the Kiss Players, Ohshima returned to the idea of the Transformers "powering up" from their human partners. But instead of physically combining with the robots — becoming their heads, guns, or engines — the Kiss Players powered-up the Transformers through *kisses* — hence the line's name.

That's right: the power of girl drawn as if she were underage would charge Optimus Prime's engines, readying him to go into battle against the Decepticons.

Because there's just nothing like romantic contact with girls to

---

[5] Of course, manga are illustrated in as many different styles as American comics or any other visual art, but because the large-eyed, sometimes childish style common to many manga is so different from most Western art, it's become identified with all manga.

make the body of an extraterrestrial war machine flood with energy.

Now, we could well imagine a relatively benign — if not actually innocent — version of this concept, in which the Transformers are combined with big-eyed manga girls, who give those Transformers little kisses.

But then you see the figures. And how they're posed in promotional photographs. And the art on the box. And the fiction.

The front of the box for the Convoy x Melissa toy.

Consider the toy for Optimus Prime (known as Convoy in Japan), who's packaged with a girl named Melissa — who was supposedly the character Marissa Faireborn, who'd appeared infrequently in the third season of the G1 cartoon show — although she'd never been depicted as looking this young. Optimus Prime is marginalized on his own box, in favor of a blonde girl in her panties sticking her butt out towards the viewer. Her mouth and eyes are open wide, suggesting shock and alarm.

It's interesting how Melissa is depicted, since she's the one character who's clearly intended to be White – not only because she originated on the cartoon show but because she's blonde. She's depicted in an assemblage of American tropes that seem incongruent, at least to American eyes. She's leaning against a surfboard, suggesting surfer culture, but she's wearing a cross necklace and a black-and-pink top with a cutesy skull design, which seems to combine Barbie-style girlishness with goth / emo traits. Her surfboard colors echo this black and pink palette. While it's not impossible to imagine a devout Christian surfer girl who loves Barbie but gets her clothes at Hot Topic, these aren't subcultures that usually mix.

The toy included a plastic version of the Optimus Prime Binaltech mold, the engine block that transforms into a gun from the Binaltech mold, plus the PVC figure of Melissa with two sets of unmovable arms and two sets of unmovable feet (so that she could be posed either sitting in / on the car or else standing or leaning over suggestively like in the illustration on the front of the box), her surf board (which transformed into a sword), and a CD containing the first five episodes of the *Kiss Players* audio drama and the bonus audio story "Someday, Beneath the Sun," starring Convoy and Melissa (all in Japanese, of course) – in which he rescues her while she swims from a tentacled monster.

Curiously, the next Kiss Players toy was a one-off in a very different style, but still featuring a Transformer and a girl: a bespeckled Japanese companion named Atari, who dressed in a fetishistic sailor outfit (perhaps echoing the popular anime *Sailor Moon*). Her unmovable figurine was larger than the ones for the rest of the line[6] and was positioned sitting on the ground as if

---

[6] This makes her figure incompatible with the main line, which is a bit odd given that the line uses Binaltech molds, which were unique in their focus on keeping a consistent scale.

frightened by something. Her Transformer companion was an Autorooper, which in Kiss Players continuity was one of the mass-produced government-controlled robots who had the same body design as Jazz (known as Meister in Japan). In theory, each had its own Kiss Players companion. Curiously, this version of Autorooper had been shrunk, so that the usual size difference between the Transformer and the girl is inverted with this release! The toy came with a CD containing the next five episodes of the *Kiss Players* audio drama and a short bonus audio story entitled "Atari-chan's Critical Moment!?", in which Autorooper shrinks and enters Atari's body, *Fantastic Voyage*-style – thereby lending a fictional justification for the odd toy.

The next release returned to the Convoy scale and style, and it was none other than Hot Rod (known as Hot Rodimus in Japan), now paired with Syaosyao, a Chinese girl who knew kung-fu. As such, the front of the box features her in a traditional red Chinese dress, shouting aggressively as she performs a kick. We might find this refreshing, compared to the helplessness of Melissa's depiction... except that she's shot from underneath and is wearing (for some reason) a padlocked metal collar!

The Hot Rodimus figure was a retool of the Alternators figure for Mirage, which had only been released in the states – making this a new mold to the Japanese market. Because Kiss Players figures were cast in plastic, instead of Binaltech's metal, this was the only toy mold from the line that was *both* released in Japan and only released in plastic.[7] The new head, created for this retool, even featured a retractable visor (imitating the one Hot Rod uses in the animated *Transformers: The Movie*).

The toy also includes the engine block from the Mirage release; it splits apart and transforms into either two guns or two tonfa weapons (batons with a T-shaped side handle). New for this release was a fishing rod for Hot Rod (reminiscent of how he fished in

---

[7] A couple additional molds were American exclusives, never released in Japan. In 2007, the American version of the line released this Hot Rod as a San Diego Comic-Con exclusive – although it lacked Syaosyao or any of the new accessories added for the Kiss Players release.

Transformers: The Movie) that transforms into a four-barrel blaster (reminiscent of the pipes that ran alongside his G1 car mode). Unlike Melissa, Syaosayo's figure doesn't come with alternate arms and legs, leaving her permanently in a seated position that... reveals her panties. Syaosyao comes with a steamer for buns, with one bun on top of it and a separate detachable bun. The included CD contained the next ten episodes of the *Kiss Players* audio drama and the bonus audio story "Tonight's Big Catch?", starring Hot Rod and Syaosyao.

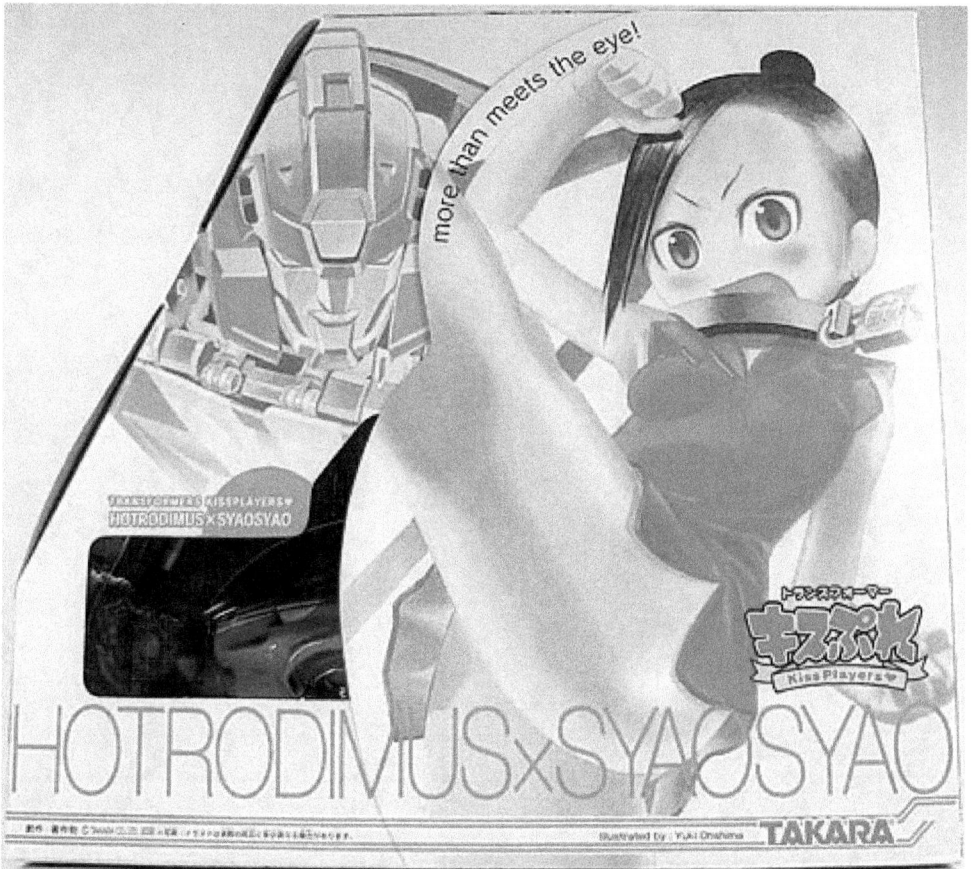

The front of the box for the Hot Rodimus x Syaosyao toy.

The final release in this style was Autorooper and Atari, who'd already been released in that strange one-off toy where their usual size differential was reversed. On the front of this box, we see Atari, wearing the same glasses and sailor outfit as before, in distress due to an electrical gremlin of sorts that is *emerging from her crotch*. (Because girls' crotches are filled with dangerous energy.) Officially, this gremlin was the sentient electric entity Kremzeek, introduced in season two of the G1 cartoon show (in the episode "Kremzeek," which even left him in Japan) – although he'd never shown this kind of interest in humans before.

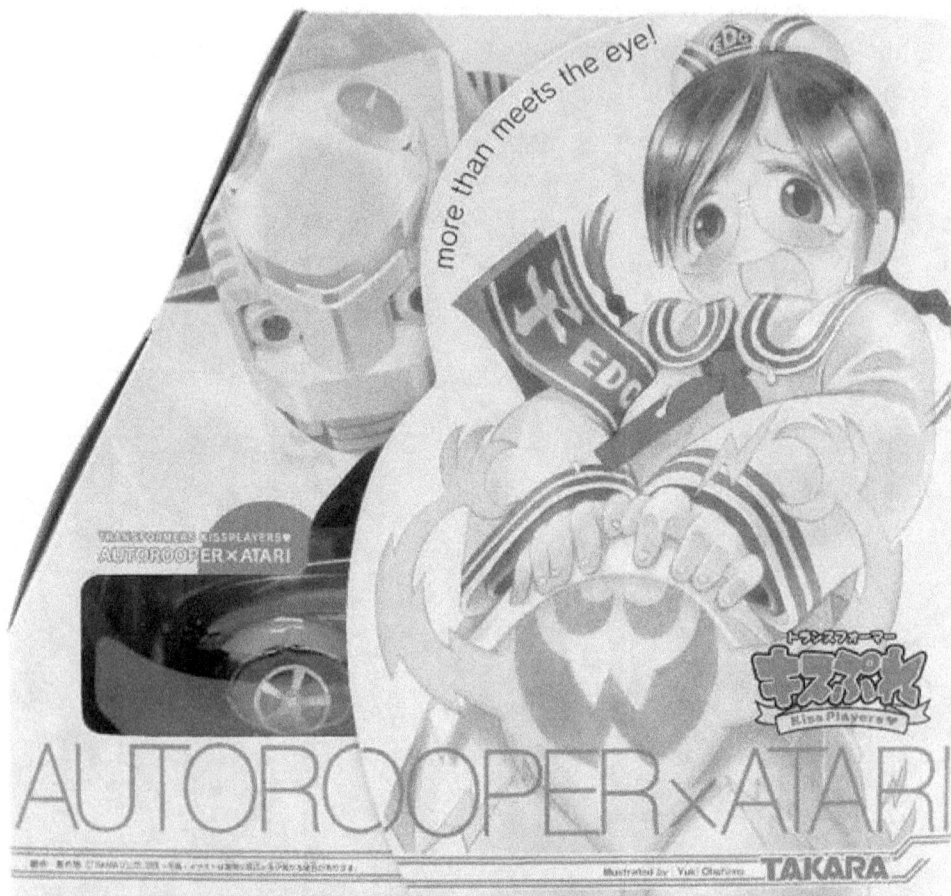

The front of the box for the Autorooper x Atari toy.

The Autorooper toy was a retool of the Binaltech mold for Jazz (called Meister in Japan). It includes, from that earlier mold, the detaching muffler that turns into a gun. Because Autrooper turned into a police car and Toyko had 48 Autorooper units, the toy included stickers so the car could be styled as any of these 48 units or as a standard Japanese police car. New for this release were four traffic cones which, piled atop each other, turned into a blaster weapon. Unlike Melissa, this Atari figurine (now scaled properly) didn't feature alternate legs, so that she had to remain seated, but she did feature an alternate set of arms holding a barf bag (playing off her girlish helplessness, her character suffered from motion sickness). The toy also included a Kremzeek figurine.

Marissa / Melissa, from the inside of the front flap
of the box for the Convoy x Melissa toy.

Ignoring their problematic content, these were impressive toys. At the time, only the earliest entries in Takara's Masterpiece line – an expensive line featuring G1 designs and focused on adult collectors, often with accessories based on cartoon episodes or the animated movie – had been released. Mainline releases were still often simplistic and rarely included the number of accessories common to Kiss Players.

The boxes were also impressively designed, arguably works of art in themselves – asymmetrical, with a slice taken out of their upper-left corner, their palette united by their light, pastel colors, and original art or big photos spreads on almost every side. The box's front features the girl on a flap, which opens to give a better view, through a plastic window, of the toys inside. There's another image of the girl on the inside of the flap.

On Optimus Prime's / Convoy's box, opening the flap gives you another view of Marissa / Melissa, in some... very tight panties, *taking off her shirt*. She's blushing and sweating, drawn in a way that makes it looks like she might be crying. She's obviously shy or alarmed for some unknown reason. This isn't a depiction of someone happy to be undressing. Is some off-panel Decepticon forcing her to do this? Or is Optimus Prime?

The boxes also distort the original meaning of the Transformers motto, "More than Meets the Eye!" Originally, that signified how these were "Robots in Disguise" – robots who could masquerade as human vehicles. Now, "More than Meets the Eye!" appears on the boxes in a soft, feminine arc along the edge of the front flap – as if suggesting that, when you open the flap, you're getting at what lay beneath. It's clear that the classic phrase is being deliberately played with, suggesting the sexual content barely masked behind the veil of innocent kissing.

On the left side of the box, which had a slice cut out of it, an Autobot symbol-shaped window let potential buyers peer into the box from another angle. Under this, each box had an image of the girl kissing the robot in the box – the one place on the box that the "power up" function of the Kiss Players is depicted. Thus, we get Optimus himself, getting his charge of power from his particularly empassioned girl companion.

Marissa / Melissa kisses Optimus Prime / Convoy,
from the side of the box for the Convoy x Melissa toy.

Kiss Players didn't last long, after these initial few releases in 2006. In 2007, the line had three final releases, all of them exclusives and none of them featuring vehicles or anything else in the Binaltech scale. These included two sets that each featured three recolored versions of unrelated, tiny, earlier toys,[8] and a recolored version of the larger Atari PVC figure called Atariscream and meant to represent Atari's possession by Starscream's ghost. By then, the movie line was arriving, and the Kiss Players line ended with only a few toys released.

---

[8] The first set were animals that folded into spheres and had a keychain attached. The molds went back to 1988 and had already been reused in 1998 as part of Takara's *Beast Wars* line. The second set were recolored versions of G1 cassettes.

Later, in 2009, Takara launched a related line called Alternity, similarly consisting of licensed, real-world cars, many of them G1 characters in new bodies. Like Binaltech, these would all be in the same scale — only this time, that scale would be 1:32 instead of 1:24. This might be justified by the desire to later include larger, military vehicles.[9] But only four molds (and a lot of repaints) were released through 2012.

The next year, the line continued as Transformers GT, a small line mostly consisting of the Alternity mold for Optimus Prime, now retooled as a racing car and repainted to represent four different characters. The story behind this was that the two Transformers factions had put down their arms in favor of competing in an annual race. In a move recalling Binaltech Asterisk and Kiss Players, Transformers GT molds came with girl figures. This time, these figures were retools of the 2005 Micro Sister figure from Takara's Microman line. This meant they were fully posable (unlike Binaltech Asterisk and Kiss Players figurines), but it also meant that they were far too large to fit in the cars with which they were packaged! Officially, these girls represented the models hired to promote racing sponsors that are common to motorsports.

So the Kiss Players didn't get that many toys, and neither did its successor lines. But back in 2006, it was supported by not only the audio stories included on those CDs but with a manga series. The audio stories had their own problematic content, but it wasn't visual. So it's not surprising that the manga would seem worse, but the manga seemed to take joy in deliberately pushing the pedophilic edge.

Of course, the manga wasn't allowed to feature explicit nudity or actual sex, but it certainly contained a large amount of sexually evocative imagery. Almost any excuse was used to splatter the scantily-clad girls with something resembling white fluid. The girls frequently were shown cowering in fear, blushing and teary-eyed, backed against walls in suggestive postures, butts raised in the air.

---

[9] Curiously, most Masterpiece cars, after the line's scale was reset in 2011 with its second version of Optimus Prime (MP-10), were around a 1:32 scale.

Optimus Prime, infused by Marissa following a kiss, seems to menace a frightened, near naked Atari.

For example, one page features Atari, all but nude, her sailor uniform ripped, wearing only her panties from her torso down, looking shocked and scared her arms fearfully covering her breasts, and her back arched to shove her ass out towards the approaching Transformer — which, in this case, is none other than Optimus Prime in his Binaltech body. The apparently nude girl who appears like a ghost inside him is Marissa — her appearance a visual representation of how one of the Kiss Players has used the power of a kiss to literally combine with a Transformer, powering him up.

If you recall, Kiss Players continued from Binaltech, which was set in the five-year gap that, in Japanese continuity, sits between the animated movie and season three of the original cartoon. During this time, Galvatron's body, after Rodimus Prime punched him out of Unicron during the movie, collided with Earth, causing some of his Unicron-powered "cells" to disperse through the atmosphere. When they merged with people, these cells turned some people into Kiss Players, capable of powering up Transformers.[1] Within the comic, this is depicted as the Kiss Player standing naked inside the Transformer — and they escape by the Transformer *vomiting* them up, naked and slimy.

But these Unicron-infused cells also merged with other things, creating Legions — monsters who looked suspiciously like the G1 Megatron and who seemed to have a penchant for binding and eating girls. They would serve as the antagonists in Kiss Players stories, popping up whenever a story needed to menace the Kiss Players or others.

In one sequence, a Legion has captured Syaosyao, keeping her bound in little more than her underwear and her locked collar. As she watches helplessly, he devours a human, and the victim's guts seem to spill over her, flowing down her body. But the guts are drawn like any other fluid, are white in the black-and-white art, and are in one close-up shown splashed across her wide-eyed face.

---

[1] The Kiss Players program was run by Earth Defense Command, the same organization that had built the Autoroopers by reverse-engineering Galvatron's body.

After merging through the Kiss Players process, an Autorooper ejects a slimy, nude (except for her locked collar) Syaosyao by vomiting her up – on top of Atari.

Legion holds Syaosyao captive.

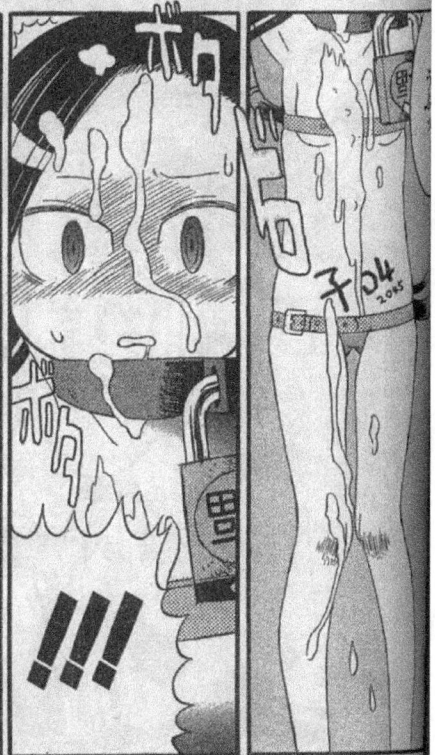

Legion eats a human, spilling the guts suggestively over his prisoner.

But Legion is most known for his very peculiar *tongue* – which acts like a long, veiny, obviously phallic tentacle. This plays on the long-standing motif of tentacle rape – although that motif is normally associated more with pornography than ostensibly kid-friendly toy lines. In Legion's case, his tentacle tongue, which looks suspiciously organic for a robot, even has a urethra and seems wet, splattering some kind of ambiguous fluid all about. Legion often thrusts it out towards the girls, implying a threat of rape.

A Legion menaces Atari.

A Legion thrusts his prehensile tongue out towards Atari.

In its second year, when the Kiss Players toy line released only old toys in different colors, the tone of the storyline softened radically, eliminating these suggestive and horror elements. Instead, the three recolored G1 cassettes released as a set formed a band with the three human girls from the first year. The band's name was the Kiss Players.

It's easy to dismiss the entire Kiss Players line as "those silly Japanese." That's certainly how it was covered in the West, where stories of young women's panties being sold in vending machines have proliferated. In fact, the Japanese I've known will tell you they've never seen such a vending machine. For as many urban legends about young Japanese women prostituting themselves to earn the money to purchase the newest technology, we can also point to young American women earning money through online sex work. Anything that seems different about a foreign culture, even if it's anecdotal and rare, becomes exaggerated abroad. And it's important to point out that there was a backlash *in Japan* against the Kiss Players. Some even complained the series was ruining their childhood memories of the Transformers characters – but then, that's been true of every Transformers line since the animated movie!

In the U.S., coverage of the Kiss Players was limited mostly to the internet. (If you look around the internet, you can find plenty of fan-made images of Optimus Prime posed with his female figurine. Her sitting on his face, for example.) Surprisingly, cable news never got hold of the story, even after the live-action movie became a huge success, just a single year later. Online, some have been offended by the Kiss Players, while others have justified it as a product of a specific Japanese cultural context. I'm pretty sure both Hasbro and Takara would rather forget it.

To me, Kiss Players is a weird sidenote to my beloved Binaltech line. It's one of the many odd bits of Transformers content produced for the Japanese market – most of which have pretty terrible fiction attached, with a lot of silly or illogical elements, but none of which (despite our stereotypes) are salacious. But as oddities go, you have to admit that it's truly remarkable to think that, just one year before the live-action movie scored at the box office, the Autobots, including the original G1 Optimus Prime, was busy – in the main Japanese line, no less – powering up by kissing girls, merging with their nude bodies, and defending other screaming girls, in their underwear and splattered with various fluids, from implied tentacle rape by a villain who looked like the G1 Megatron.[*]

---

[*] An earlier version of this article was published on the Literary Escort Services website in 2008, was republished on Martian Lit's website in Sept 2012, and was again republished on Sequart Organization's website in June 2014. It was greatly revised for this edition.

Why I Dig Michael Bay's Transformers Movie Trilogy

Mocking the live-action Transformers movies has been fashionable since the very first one. In part, that's due to their director, Michael Bay, who's got a reputation for big explosions and superficial plots – traits that seem to get worse, the more control over a project he has. When someone wants to mock Hollywood blockbusters, and they don't want to mock super-heroes, it's a fair bet that they'll mention giant robots blowing things up, or some other description that could apply to the Transformers movies.

Really, that's just a sign of those movies' commercial success. And I'm not going to argue that they're deeply philosophical movies. However, they largely deliver what's reasonable to expect from a big-budget blockbuster that's not trying to be a philosophical art-house movie: specifically, some amazing action sequences, which are meaningful because they're illustrations of bigger ideas, mixed with some really good character moments.

Transformers (2007)

Let's start with the first live-action film, 2007's *Transformers*. Admittedly, part of the joy of the movie was seeing live-action Transformers in the first place – something fans had dreamed about for years, but which hadn't been technologically feasible until a few years before the movie's release.

Equally, some of the potentially embarrassing aspects of the Transformers – such as their adoption of English vernacular and human voices – are on display here, but objecting to them is a little like objecting to super-hero costumes; they're part of the tradition, for better or worse. Similarly, you can nitpick that the Transformers' adoption of human vehicle forms doesn't make sense, but that's kind of like pointing out that super-powers aren't realistic. A lot of these are simply aspects of the premise itself. The movie doesn't execute these things perfectly – I'd certainly like a little more explanation, and these movies' sci-fi narration can be ponderous (like much opening and closing narration in sci-fi and super-hero movies).

But Bay does get some things right, like trying to retain the Transformers' scale between their forms – something the original comics and cartoon often got very wrong, prompting theories to explain the discrepancies. (I say "Bay" and not the screenwriters, because this rule was reportedly set at Bay's insistence.) Bay also helped invent the idea that, since the Transformers could transform, they didn't need a ship, and thus we see the Autobots coming to Earth in forms resembling meteors. Bay would later use Transformers ships, but the meteor-like "protoform" idea was a solid way of thinking through and working out the Transformers premise.

The movie was executive produced by Stephen Spielberg, and he contributed in meaningful ways to the film. Spielberg chose the screenwriters, decided that the story should be grounded in a boy and his car, reviewed and gave notes on drafts of the script, and asked Michael Bay to direct the film. It's not too much to say that the film is divided between Spielberg and Bay, between character-driven moments focused around Sam Witwicky (the Spielberg side of the equation) and giant action pieces (the Bay influence).

And here's the thing: both of these sides of the movie work *really well*. Their combination gives the action a soul, and it also solves the problem of what you do in a Transformers movie between giant, super-expensive action scenes.

Shia LaBeouf takes a lot of critical flak, some of it deserved (both for his acting and for his off-screen life). But he's *brilliant* as a young man nervous about getting the girl, anxious about his fiances, and focused on getting the gorgeous girl.

Watching the movie, I'm always reminded of 1980s movies, like *License to Drive* (1988) or even *Ferris Beuller's Day Off* (1986). It was an era when Billy Ocean could sing "Get out of my Dreams, Get into My Car" (1988), as if the two went hand-in-hand. The car has long been a symbol of America, but those movies sold a particular combination of the car and the young American heterosexual male, at a particular point in his life, when high school still seems like the world and romantic success – especially for a kid who isn't rich – can seem painfully wedded to something like having a cool car. We haven't seen many movies since the 1980s that have really sold the magic of a young, naturally lustful man and his car. In fact, I'm not sure how well those 1980s movies really sold this as a coherent formula. But man, does *Transformers* sell it – and man, does it work.

Of course, the 1980s were also the era in which the Transformers were born, and the story of Sam Witwicky adapts a story that began in the closing pages of *Transformers* #1 (Sept 1984), in which the young Witwicky – there named Buster – encounters Bumblebee leaking fuel and speaking in his father's garage. It's a haunting image. The movie wisely removes the father's job as a mechanic, and it replaces this setting for a used car lot, where Sam's choice of Bumblebee is rooted both in his family's limited, middle-class income and the idea that the right car, like the right girl, could literally or figuratively speak to you.

This reinvigoration of 1980s tropes is handled with great acting and great visual panache, but I won't deny that it's in some ways a throwback – and not only to the glory days of the American automotive industry. The middle-class, all-American young man defining himself by his car and his girlfriend, which are treated similarly and packaged together, carries undeniable sexist and racial overtones. Sam's the white male good guy, with whom we identify despite his white lies, and his would-be girlfriend, Mikaela Banes (played by Megan Fox), is defined by her sexiness just as much as the car is. This is true despite the fact that Mikaela does get some important moments of interiority, in which we realize that she's struggling painfully with her own family and class issues, which are actually in excess of Sam's domestic obstacles. But while anyone would be foolish to deny these overtones, we'd also be foolish to deny how well these tropes of the girl and the car and the nervous heterosexual white boy are welded together into a whole that, through its acting and its visuals, has that elusive movie magic to a remarkable extent.

Everything that happens with Sam, Mikaela, and Sam's parents is infused with the concerns of his story. When the Autobots stand in his yard and Sam tries to keep them out of sight, it's humorous enough on its own. But it's also about Sam desperate to juggle the various parts of his life. He feels like he has to pretend to be someone else to win Mikaela, and he's soon hiding what he's doing with the Autobots from his parents. That the Transformers are tied to Sam's ancestor, the explorer Archibald Witwicky, is accomplished through the somewhat silly idea of information being etched on Archibald's glasses. But this demonstrates how, as in the best action movies, everything that happens is an illustration of the protagonist's mental state. The Transformers themselves are bound up in Sam's family history, just as his discovery of Bumblebee is bound up in his family's limited budget. Everything's of a piece here.

The more traditional Michael Bay parts of the film also work exceptionally well. Sure, the movie films its soldiers like it's filming pornography, and there's a fascist worship of the military that underlies this. But we're hardly talking about *300* or anything, and the soldiers in question are real heroes, who act selfishly. And the action sequences are terrific.

There's a reason the sequence in which Blackout lands without a pilot, on a base in Qatar, then dramatically transforms and kills almost everyone there, was used in trailers for the movie. It's tense, stunning stuff. Viewers know what the Transformers are, but the humans don't. And when we first see them, both this reveal and their deadly potential are handled with magnificent cinematic drama. This is hardly special effects for its own sake; its special effects wedded to human drama and a sequence that uses cinema's strengths, rather than substitutes for them.

Of course, when discussing the Michael Bay action half of the movie, nothing beats the climax, in which the conflict moves to a fictional American city. True, the explanation for this setting is a plot hole: the heroes are trying to take the Allspark (a MacGuffin, to be sure) away from the Decepticons, knowing the Decepticons are pursuing it, and they choose *a population center*. But the action that ensues is a perfect illustration of the movie's tagline "Their War, Our World." It's an idea that was always implicit in the premise of the Transformers, although the original comics and cartoon pulled its punches and never depicted the kind of urban decimation that would actually happen, were the Transformers actually battling on

Earth. What we get in the movie's climax isn't just some thrilling devastation. It's actually the fulfillment of the entire Transformers premise – a fulfillment earlier incarnations of the Transformers weren't brave enough to stage.

When we see a missile from a Decepticon plane slamming into a skyscraper, it's not just entertaining carnage and mayhem. It's a courageous willingness to follow through on the implications of the story. In cinemas less than six years after 9/11 (and years before the devastation seen in *The Avengers* or *Man of Steel*), this kind of urban devastation could be difficult to watch. But how lame would the movie have been, if giant robots had carried their war to Earth, only to battle only in conveniently secluded areas? It was mind-bending to see Transformers realistically swerving down populated streets. But the easy damage they inflict on everything they touch also demonstrates a laudable willingness to follow a story's central premise to its logical conclusion, rather than rely on narrative dodges.

On both the human, Spielberg level and the action-packed, Bay level, *Transformers* accomplishes impressive feats. Sure, there are a million things I can nitpick. (Beyond what I've already mentioned, Frenzy is a bit too silly, and I've never liked the over-intricate surfaces of the Transformers' robot forms. And while much of the acting is excellent, especially those playing the Witwicky family, John Turturro and Jon Voight aren't given very interesting characters.) *Transformers* isn't a perfect movie by any means. But it's a good action movie, with several stunningly good sequences. In some very important ways, it improves on existing Transformers lore.

It's more than a good action movie. It's an admirable one.

Revenge of the Fallen (2009)

Say what you want about the Transformers sequels – and I'll say plenty of good *and* bad things below. They were directed by the original movie's director, Michael Bay, executive produced by Stephen Spielberg, and represented different stages of protagonist Sam Witwicky's life – as portrayed by Shia LaBeouf in each film. *Transformers* (2007) showed Sam as a high-school student.

Transformers: Revenge of the Fallen (2009) showed Sam in college. And *Transformers: Dark of the Moon* (2011) showed Sam struggling on the post-college job market. Each time, Sam was struggling to form his own identity, during these periods of an American man's life, and each time he was played by the same actor.

How many action franchises can you say this about? Richard Donner directed one and a half Superman movies. Tim Burton directed two Batman movies. Christopher Nolan got three Batman movies, all with the same actor, and got to end his story — for which he's been understandably applauded. But whatever you think about the relative merits of their films, Transformer director Michael Bay did this — and stayed for two *more* installments. Jon Favreau only made it through two Iron Man films, while Joss Whedon and Zack Snyder got through two Avengers movies and two and a half DC movies, respectively.

The idea of depicting a different stage in a young man's life with each film is something we'd normally associate with art-house films, not big-budget, sci-fi blockbusters. No, I'm not claiming these three films are art films, but what they're doing, in relation to one another, is something ambitious and admirable. That's arguably Hollywood at its best, able to fuse popular content with deeper structures and meanings.

And if it matters, all three Transformers movie have grossed more than the one before, with *Dark of the Moon* surpassing a billion dollars worldwide.

But first came *Revenge of the Fallen*, which… isn't a good movie. It has some excellent ideas, but they're unfortunately buried within a jumble of material that rarely works at all.

The movie tries to duplicate the formula for the first film, which so ably blended its Spielbergian tale of a high-school boy and his car with big-scale action sequences. Only here, the Sam Witwicky story largely doesn't work. Sam is away at college and struggling to keep his high-school relationship with Mikeala Banes going. When the Decepticons resurface, Sam's college life is interrupted, and the opportunity this provides for heroism allows him and Mikaela to reconnect. That's not a lot to work with, and his arc mostly feels like a retread of the first movie. Like many sequels, instead of carrying the protagonist's story forward, he's given a setback between films, so that returning to the new status quo achieved at the end of the first film can feel like an accomplishment.

Moreover, the movie isn't successful in grounding Sam's second arc in college, the way his arc in the first film was grounded in high-school anxieties and concerns. True, we're shown Sam adjusting to college life, leaving his girlfriend and Bumblebee behind. When Sam's seduced by a Decepticon in human form – a reinvention of the Pretender concept from the original toy line – it's supposed to be an illustration of the sexual temptations faced by residential undergraduates, which *can* make long-distance relationships with high-school partners difficult. But it's all too titillating, all too quickly dismissed, and a little too head-on to have the deeper resonance it could have. Similarly, when we see Sam struggling in a classroom, it's not because he's an adolescent with normal college problems but because he's hallucinating, due to his exposure to the AllSpark. And yes, it's a little amusing to see Transformers fighting on a college campus, but none of this captures the anxieties of this period in a young American man's life, the way the first film did with high school.

The movie soon leaves college behind, as if it can't wait to focus on its action-driven plot. Unfortunately, this too is a let-down. Optimus Prime is (temporarily) killed, a development that was first depicted in the 1986 animated movie and which has recurred often enough that it's become a trope of Transformers stories. The removal of Optimus Prime raises the stakes for the survivors and ostensibly allows Sam to find his courage in the absence of Optimus Prime's leadership. But Optimus's death feels more perfunctory than dramatic.

One of the conceits of the films is that each of them reveal some previous interaction between Transformers and Earth. Rather than changing human history from what we recognize, these interactions *produce* the human history we know. This plays into the fad for conspiracy theories, especially those about alien-human contact, and the movies have a decent amount of fun with this.

In the first film, Earth is where the AllSpark fell – and where Megatron, searching for it, got frozen in ice. This led to the creation of Sector 7, a secret American governmental organization that knew the truth and was meant to prepare for any future alien incursions. The movie also revealed that Hoover Dam was built partly to house the dormant Megatron and the AllSpark. This irritates me slightly: the Hoover Dam was one of the largest public works projects in history, and it ought to be lionized as such, especially given America's ahistorical contempt for the idea that government can do much of anything. More annoying is the idea that cellular phones and the like have been reverse-engineered from Transformer technology, an idea that simultaneously mystifies and devalues the real work of scientists, while also radically exaggerating our ability to reverse-engineer anything from truly alien technology. But whatever. These are common enough sci-fi tropes, and I'm able to overlook their annoying implications.

In *Revenge of the Fallen*, we learn that the ancient Transformer known as the Fallen — the founder of the Decepticons — ruled ancient Egypt, yet apparently had use of human slaves despite the vastly superior technology available to him. The absurd idea that aliens built the Pyramids has become a stable of irresponsible alternate history, which makes it almost pardonable. But it's all rather convoluted, to say the least. There are Sun Harvesters, including one hidden inside one of the Pyramids of Giza (which has somehow gone undetected all these years). There's also the Tomb of the Primes, and the idea that noble Transformers would transform into walls to enclose a great secret is a cool one — except that it's not clear why they'd have to die to do so, and it's all bound up in another mystical Transformers MacGuffin, the Matrix. The idea that Transformers history, at such a key point, had already intersected so heavily with Earth's, feels like a mistake, but the idea that Earth's location would somehow be lost to the Transformers is utterly absurd. None of this makes sense, despite some interesting ideas at work.

And that's very much the problem with *Revenge of the Fallen*: tons of ideas, many of them good, but none of them explored. It's the Transformers version of the problem that plagues many superhero sequels, in which too many villains and plots are crammed together — with the result being a mess in which none of them shines, rather than an epic feeling.

Jetfire's a perfect example. His design is pretty fantastic, and the idea of a Transformer in the form of an SR-71 Blackbird hiding in the Air and Space Museum is frankly awesome. But when did he acquire this form? Why is he in the museum? Is it even possible to imagine, as the movie requires, that he's been hanging out on Earth since ancient Egypt?

But above all other examples of this overstuffed effect is the introduction of whole new classes of Transformers — concepts familiar to Transformers fans but that any one of which would be more than enough for a single film. You have the Pretenders, recast here as Transformers able to assume human form (or at least the form of hot co-eds?). It's an ability with vast implications (e.g., the Decepticons could impersonate the President of the United States), totally ignored by this and later movies. Then you have the idea of combiners: the fact that the Constructicons can unite to form the giant robot Devastator. In the climax, we're casually introduced to yet another concept: that a Transformer could become body armor as a way of souping up someone else. Here's how that's introduced: a dying Jetfire says, "Take my parts." Optimus Prime does, as if anyone would know how to do this and it's no surprise that Jetfire's compatible in this way. Optimus then goes flying off, rather morbidly wearing Jetfire's corpse. If the movie hadn't jumped the shark already, it surely does at this moment.

As if all of this wasn't enough, the voices and personalities of Mudflap and Skids seemed to embody racist stereotypes. I'm sure the filmmakers thought these "humorous" personalities were just a bit of fun, parallel to many Transformers' unique voices and silly personalities, but these two characters' portrayal recalled the (rather obvious, I thought) problems with Jar Jar Binks and was uncomfortable to watch. It also compounds the problem that Jazz was the only Autobot killed in the first movie, which suggested that the racist trope of the black character(s) dying is so strong that it even applies in a movie about robots from outer space. Instead of making this an anomaly, the sequel seems to double-down on the strategy of using robots as a shield for some pretty troubling racial depictions. I'm sure someone in Hollywood is okaying these depictions as examples of diversity, but with all the complaints they've received, it's time for them to stop.

It's not only critics who have panned the film. To their credit, many of the movie's creators have agreed. Michael Bay said the criticism was fair, singled out the Fallen as a poor villain, blamed the 2007-2008 writers' strike for problems with the script, and resolved to do better with the third film. Lorenzo Di Bonaventurra isolated one of the core problems, saying, "We tried to do too many things in the second movie, which didn't give enough time in any one of them. We were constantly jumping to the next piece of information, the next place." Shia LaBeouf agreed, saying the movie had lost its human core while trying to outdo the action of the original. This kind of honesty and public recognition of a movie's failings is pretty rare, especially for a movie that was a stunning commercial success.

Fortunately, the third film would be much better.

Dark of the Moon (2011)

Despite its strange title, *Dark of the Moon* represented a return to form for the series and managed to push both its human and Transformers plots into brave new territory.

We've looked at how the 2007 movie embodied high-school male anxieties of Sam Witwicky, weaving them pretty intricately into the movie's plot. We've also examined how the 2009 sequel only superficially addressed Sam's transition to college life. Both of those periods in a young man's life have been addressed often enough before. *Dark of the Moon* places Sam in far less familiar territory, as he enters the post-college job market.

Sam's joining the American labor force at a very specific time in American economic history. After the crash of 2008, Wall Street recovered within a few years, and economic data indicated that the recession – at least as officially measured – was over. The affluent have remained just as wildly prosperous as before, and the aspects of the economy that cater to them (such as the high-end housing market) have done very well during the recovery. But Main Street still hasn't recovered, and employment numbers have improved at a painfully slow pace. The gap between the rich and the poor keeps relentlessly expanding, and the middle class feel themselves to be slipping backwards, with more and more people struggling and unable to make ends meet, or being forced to take steps such as living with their parents in order to build any kind of economic foundation under their feet. Data shows that class mobility has for decades been weaker in the U.S. than most industrialized nations. The American Dream increasingly seems like an outdated notion, as the vast majority of Americans adjust their expectations downward.

This is reflected in the movie in Sam's difficulty finding a job and in his class envy towards Dylan Gould, for whom his girlfriend, Carly Spencer, works. Gould embodies the American upper crust. His offices are super-modern. He collects expensive cars — a hobby not only indicative of extreme wealth but tied into the theme of the Transformers. Gould is a high-flyer with powerful connections. He's slick, well-dressed, and happy... because he can afford to be. He's also arrogant — although he sees himself as a good guy and promotes the idea that he is. To Sam's consternation, Carly buys into Gould's self-promotion — which represents how getting a paycheck so often corrupts our mentality, bending us towards the ideology of our apparent benefactors.

Gould is Donald Trump. He's Gordon Gecko. And of course, he's ultimately the human villain of the piece, who sees a Decepticon victory as inevitable and wants to get his piece of the action. It's a particularly capitalistic bit of rationalizing. The good of the planet, or the species — whether the issue is climate change or a Decepticon takeover — isn't something the capitalist drive for profit is equipped to tackle. In the movie's final act, Gould becomes a bit too two-dimensional for my taste, but it's not hard to see how he could see a Decepticon takeover as an arbitrage opportunity. Indeed, we've seen what was once considered war profiteering become commonplace and even something that's applauded in certain circles.

Gould is also an antidote to the wealthy, supposedly benevolent protagonists of many big-budget action movies. From Batman to Iron Man, we've often been made to identify with the wealthy and powerful – and to forgive their many mistakes and eccentricities because they're depicted as the good guys, as smart visionaries who will always be in the right, even when they're so obviously in the wrong. Gould's not a perfect character, but he's a breath of fresh air.

Sam's relationship with Carly also reflects another timely issue: that women are making more money. The old idea of husbands as breadwinner isn't quite dead yet, but it's certainly on its way out. Recent economic downturns have seen women's incomes recover quicker, so the two issues are connected historically as well as thematically in the movie. Of course, women still make less money than men, and there's been more than a little consternation in some camps over this shift. Surely, a lot of that's simply those with power – in this case, men – expressing alarm at their declining privilege. But that's also true of anxieties about America's perceived decline. That these are privileged concerns doesn't invalidate them as subject matter for artistic exploration. In fact, many of the most beloved genre movies (*Invasion of the Body Snatchers*, *Rosemary's Baby*, etc.) reflect the anxieties of their times, and powerful movies do so ably, even when those anxieties seem more than a little silly, privileged, or paranoid in retrospect.

Yes, *Dark of the Moon* is really about the declining middle class and Sam's crisis of masculinity. And yes, the movie ends up affirming Sam's perspective, since he was *right* to be suspicious of Carly's rich boss. From this perspective, the movie may be read as a male fantasy, similar to how the original *Die Hard* ends with John McClane's estranged wife taking his last name.

Sam's experience in the film also reflects how many college graduates are naive about what an undergraduate degree means. For decades, Americans have been sold on college as a means to achieve a better job. When I've asked my own students, the vast majority say this is why they're in college. That's not what college used to be about – which is why four-year colleges still have general-education requirements designed to produce well-rounded, educated individuals, capable of critical thought, aware of how science works, and ready to participate in a democracy. College today is increasingly a business, and not only at for-profit universities (which have low success rates and huge overhead, despite what you've heard about business doing everything better). Non-profit universities are also busy replacing tenured professors with part-time adjuncts to save money, and the biggest names in American education are opening foreign branches to monetize their reputations. Meanwhile, undergraduate degrees don't get someone very far. Data shows they help in the long run – although I suspect this is mostly because people feel more confident hiring a college graduate and expect to pay that person more. But in the short run, unless your degree is in a few specialized fields, a college degree doesn't open an awful lot of doors.

Yet I've often heard from college graduates who were surprised at this. One told me he expected that an English degree meant some newspaper or publisher eagerly would hire him. In part, this is surely due to the widespread propaganda about how college leads to better jobs. Even at the most reputable schools, colleges do little to disabuse students of this notion. Most departments are desperate for enrollment. If they don't get it, classes are cancelled, salaries are affected, and you can pretty much forget any new positions, expanded course offerings, or even (in some places) office supplies. So professors tell students about how an English degree or knowing a foreign language is useful in pretty much any occupation – which is true. But students take this nebulous advice to mean that *they* will find a job after graduating... and then they're disappointed.

Heck, my father was a professor, and my undergraduate institution was all about making your *brain* better. It couldn't have cared less about whether you were going to get a job, and it bravely didn't pretend to. That was beneath its concern; that wasn't its job, as an institution. So I had few illusions on that front. But I still felt that post-graduation let-down, as I discovered that the professors who knew I was a brilliant, hard-working student weren't going to drop my name with publishers or other high-flying friends, including in major graduate departments. It's hard to realize you've climbed a tall and arduous ladder, investing huge amounts of time and money and mental energy doing so, only to discover that you're at the bottom of a whole new ladder, for which you have very little training.

And that's the situation Sam finds himself in. He's a college graduate, and no one cares. No one's opening any doors for him.

Of course, this is informed by Sam's experience in the past two movies. But instead of derailing the message, this enhances it. Sam says he saved the world twice, but he can't tell anyone – because it's a conceit of the first two movies that the Transformers' existence remains a secret, marginalized to the conspiratorial fringe.

I really love this dynamic. It augments the depiction of Sam as a freshly minted college grad, unable to find work and anxious about his masculinity. Because Sam's not just a new graduate who's excelled in high school and college. He literally *saved the world* during both these periods. It's a great metaphor for Sam's sense of his own accomplishments, of his hard work, which don't seem to matter now that it counts.

This is also a great commentary on the fact that, despite the platitudes, American capitalism isn't a meritocracy – a pain that's very dear to my own heart. In some ways, Sam's experience saving the world *hurts* him as he tries to find his place. People don't believe him, and what boss wants to hire someone who thinks he's done more for the world than all his coworkers? Many of the brightest young adults face a very similar situation, in which bosses may think they're bragging about their accomplishments and are reluctant to have a subordinate who's too smart, especially at an entry-level position. And these bosses are right to be concerned, because even if the young person is hired, he or she is likely to feel that they're under-utilized and under-appreciated, since they know what they're capable of.

This is a conundrum I know well, and I've rarely seen it reflected in a movie, let alone as well as it is in *Dark of the Moon*. As a 21-year-old college grad, I'd gotten a great education, taken my studies very seriously, graduated with honors, won an award, and had several helpful mentors. I'd also written several unpublished books, completing the first as a high-school freshman. I was in the top percentile on just about every standardized test, had grown up with childhood experts saying I was literally off their charts, and had known my I.Q. for eight years. If you grew up like I did, with movies about wunderkinds embraced by the American dream, you'd expect me to wind up at a publisher, on the writing staff of a TV show, snatched up by a talent agency, working for the government, or offered a scholarship at an Ivy League school.

Instead, even the local newspapers wouldn't take me – in multiple cities. So I wound up doing temp work, for about $7 and hour, and nothing about me mattered except that I knew Microsoft Office and could type quickly. (Ironically, these were skills I'd refined doing research and writing that now didn't count for anything.) I worked as a secretary at a low-rent psychiatrist's office that was next door to a methadone clinic and got walk-ins from people very upset the clinic next door was closed. At another job, I worked in a corporate cubicle for months on a project that got scrapped for reasons I wasn't privy to — and wasn't expected to ask about. At another job, I sold porn magazines to businessmen on their lunch breaks. At one job, my boss was younger than me, wasn't very bright, was rarely present, was a dictator when she was, and surely thought she got the job due to her innate worth. I only survived with my parents' help, wound up with an awful lot of credit-card debt on top of my student loans, and finally had a nervous breakdown in which I realized I was (no joke) going to kill myself if I didn't get into grad school.

Once I got over my humbled ego, I really didn't mind any of the work itself. There was little responsibility, my coworkers were pretty cool, and I got to experience things outside the world I knew, which (being a writer) I valued greatly. Now that I'm older, I'm able to see that I needed a little humbling. And my impression that the establishment was anything but meritocratic helped spur me to at least be happy with what I did. So I went my own way and basically decided to build my own, more meritocratic institutions. Including Sequart, which you're now reading this on. After 18 years of hard work and *tons* of truly amazing support, it's still not *quite* a happy ending, but it *is* getting there.

Why recount all of this? Because I'm *so* sick of movies that perpetuate the idea that everything will work out if you have a good heart or a smart idea. Few things could possibly more damaging to perpetuate.

In fact, if you wanted to hurt people as much as possible, you might well come up with the idea that people have a destiny tied to their intrinsic merit. It's a tempting idea, but it's one I feel ethically obliged to correct.

Don't get me wrong: talent and hard work matter, and they're necessary if you're building a business. Hard work, or at least perseverance, is necessary to graduate from college or to finish a big creative project. But talent and hard work at best win you a roll of the dice — and additional rolls, when the first few don't work out. It's *luck* that separates a Mark Zuckerberg from 99 just-as-talented, just-as-hard-working other people. And that luck includes all kinds of supports, including what opportunities your family, their connections, and their wealth provides. Without such good fortune, I not only wouldn't have made it through that post-college period, but I probably wouldn't have gotten to college in the first place. No amount of merit would have mattered. On the other hand, if I'd had more such fortune, I'd have achieved a lot more with a lot less suffering.

I've never seen this reality reflected in a big-budget movie as well as I have in *Dark of the Moon*. Sam's not the smartest or the most talented candidate, but he's saved the world twice. And it doesn't matter. Meanwhile, he sees douchebags like Gould thrive.

The fact that Sam's had advantages and good luck — including supportive middle-class parents, an absurdly beautiful and wealthy girlfriend, and the good fortune not to *die* on those two past adventures — doesn't negate the central dynamic that his merit fundamentally doesn't matter. Sure, he'd have it worse if he were a woman, or a minority, or born poor. I'd pay to see that movie. But to the extent we care about the injustices perpetrated on any group, Sam's experience that ours is not a meritocracy is a starting point, without which we can't begin to discuss greater, endemic injustices.

Because if what separates Sam from Gould isn't merit, what separates anyone from either of them might not be merit either. And what separates most women from the impossibly beautiful and wealthy Carly might *also* not be merit.

And boy, if this isn't a *rare* point of view. We're constantly spoon-fed this myth of meritocracy, as if it's a state that magically comes into being. Even most movies that celebrate someone who dies for a cause endorse the concept of meritocracy, because those characters become lionized, achieving posthumously a station they couldn't in life. Movies like *Erin Brockovich* (2000) and *The Pursuit of Happyness* (2006), while ostensibly antidotes to sexism and racism, perpetuate the underlying notion of meritocracy, in which any sexism or racism is simply a temporary problem the meritocratic universe will naturally iron out.

Dark of the Moon is an action movie, and it's not focused solely on these issues. But its depiction of present-day American capitalism is braver and more accurate than those two movies (both of which are based on true stories, selected and then altered to support a meritocratic agenda).

But there's one final reason I love the post-college Sam sequences. How often do we see heroes save the day and get a happy ending? Often enough. But we're almost never shown what happens next. Most sequels basically repeat the set-up of the original movie, and we're asked to believe that either nothing's really changed or that everything has radically changed. There's almost never any thinking through of the implications of the earlier movies.

Sam's situation, in that he can't really talk about having saved the Earth, is hardly unique to the Transformers movies. We've seen dozens of everyman characters put into similar situations, and whether because a mission is top-secret or because it occurred in a remote region, they have no evidence for what they've experienced. Perhaps they've encountered extraterrestrial life, but no one else knows it. How do you go back to normal life, after something like that?

Yet we've rarely seen this. From a purely narrative standpoint, that's both unorthodox and pretty smart. It struck me immediately, and I still admire it.

All of these issues with Sam aren't separate from the Transformers-focused plot, even if the two plots aren't as thematically interwoven as they were in the 2007 movie. Even if the good guys ultimately win, Transformers are cut down left and right, and there's little accounting for merit in some of the deaths. Also, the revered Sentinel Prime is revealed to be an Autobot traitor, paralleling Gould's role in the human plot.

There are things I don't like about this movie's Transformers plot. The threat, in which technological pillars are used to transport Cybertron into our solar system, is easy to ridicule. I'm not convinced by the plot in which Earth exiles the Autobots. Perhaps the worst problem is that Cybertron is casually destroyed in the climax – with an effect I initially thought was only meant to indicate the destruction of the planetary transport system. The film doesn't adequately convey the sense of genocide – and presumably the demise of billions. In the end, Optimus Prime executes both Megatron and Sentinel Prime, which might be forgivable if we felt he'd just lost his entire species, or if the movie led us to question his morality. Instead, it's essentially a war crime, which the movie seems to brush off as if it's not really important, or doesn't compromise Optimus Prime's heroism at all.

With all of that acknowledged, there's also an awful lot to like in this plot.

As previously discussed, each of the three movies involve a retroactively revealed past encounter between the Transformers and Earth. *Revenge of the Fallen* set this encounter in Earth's distant past, which didn't work. *Dark of the Moon* may not need another such encounter, but its version is perhaps the coolest of all three films: that the space race was inspired by an Autobot ship that crashed on the Moon. Given that the Transformers movies prominently feature conspiracy theories, the Moon landing is a resonant choice, and we're treated to a fun sequence in which the astronauts stop broadcasting, then rush over to explore an impossibly vast alien craft.

The action and special effects are particularly dramatic, this time around. In the opening sequence, we get to see a live-action version of the war on Cybertron – released in 3D no less, along with the regular 2D version. But the highlight is the sequence in the Chicago skyscrapers, in which the building is torn apart and the human characters have to navigate a sloping floor with the windows knocked out, then slide down the outside of the building. It's a stunning sequence from start to finish. There too, we see the film's denial of meritocracy, as what divides human characters who die from those who live is sometimes as simple as their random physical position (as is so often the case in actual war). Rarely have I ever been so riveted by an action sequence, and I'm not usually dazzled by action for its own sake. I still think it's one of the best action sequences ever filmed – although it abruptly ends, after Optimus Prime's defeat of Shockwave, without much of a conclusion, only for the movie to cut to a captured Bumblebee, without much of an introduction! (Unfortunately, this is a Bay trait that only gets worse, as the movies go on.)

For what it's worth, the plot's filled with references that ought to please Transformers fans. We get to see the movies' version of Shockwave. Sentinel Prime is a great character with a long history in Transformers comics and cartoons, and he's voiced by Leonard Nimoy, who voiced Galvatron in the 1986 animated movie. Even some of the elements I didn't like might deserve a partial pass for their provenance. The transportation system that brings Cybertron to Earth is called a Space Bridge, and is a new version of technology that's been important to the Transformers from the earliest years of the cartoon and the comic. The idea of bringing Cybertron to Earth originates in the three-part "The Ultimate Doom," from the first season of the original Transformers cartoon.

But the movie's plot is most notable for daring to carry forward the premise of the movies. The original idea of the Transformers, as reflected in the 2007 movie, was "Their War, Our World." In other words, these impossibly alien mechanical life forms had carried their technologically advanced war to our planet. To depict this as a polite business, without casualties, is to avoid the implications of the original premise. The 2007 movie did a good job of following this through, especially given its budgetary and technological limitations, by setting the climax in the fictional Mission City. Seeing Transformers battle in an urban environment brings the original premise home in a way we hadn't really seen before that movie. But at the end of the movie, the Transformers' existence is still a secret, due to a (frankly improbable) cover-up of what happened in Mission City. This is a central conceit of the movies, in which the Transformers have altered human history without us knowing it and are the subject of conspiracy theories.

Revenge of the Fallen doesn't move this original premise forward. Yes, one of the pyramids of the Giza plateau gets torn apart, but "their war" doesn't alter "our world" much more than that. And in the end, the Transformers are covered up once again.

But of course, this can't go on. The improbability of such (international) cover-ups increases with each movie, and there's only so much fun to be had with the idea that the truth of what everyone's watching is only known to conspiracy theories. At the same time, the very premise of the series demands that it's only going to be a matter of time before "their war" affect "our world" in fundamental, big-scale ways. (This is similar to why I've defended *X-Men: The Last Stand*, despite its far more serious faults.) You can only do these kind of contained climaxes so many times before the lack of an intersection between the Transformers and present-day human history feels like narrative cowardice.

In *Dark of the Moon*, the Decepticons conquer Chicago.

To the movie's credit, it doesn't choose a fictional location, like the first movie's Mission City. This helps bring the city's devastation home, rendering it far realer and more powerful. It's eerie, seeing Decepticon ships patrolling the skies above the city's canals. It certainly feels like an alien invasion.

The Decepticons' rule looks like a military occupation. The conquest of Chicago is absolutely brutal, and the protagonists' journey into the occupied city and battle within it feels far more like a war movie than a sanitized action blockbuster. If there's one thing Michael Bay's universally acknowledged to be good at, besides explosions, it's filming military sequences. And to the movie's credit, all of Chicago is shot like a battleground.

In other words, "Their War, Our World."

By the end of the trilogy, we've seen the fulfillment of the original movie's premise. We've also followed Sam Witwicky through three distinct stages of his life. And things have changed: Cybertron's been destroyed, and there's no going back. There's also no hiding the Transformers' existence, after what we've seen in Chicago.

Dark of the Moon has some heights that exceed those of the 2007 original, but the human and Transformers plots aren't quite as wedded as they are there. Nonetheless, *Dark of the Moon* is a gripping action movie that compares favorably to the vast majority of big-budget action films.

I first saw it in 3D, and I was riveted through most of it. I've rarely had so much fun at a movie. An awful lot of the action was just mind-blowing to see. And for every bit that feels a little misjudged or unnecessary, there's another bit that feels brave to me... and far better done than probably anyone has a right to expect from a billion-dollar blockbuster.

Considered together, the original three Transformers movies certainly aren't art films, and they're an odd mix of really smart and really dumb elements. But they do tell a consistent, unified, and fascinating story that deserves far more critical acclaim than they've gotten.

No, they didn't displace the original cartoon and comic as the "definitive" version of the Transformers produced to date. But their remix of elements from all past versions of the Transformers feels as close as any other version has come.

Later Films

Unfortunately, Bay's two subsequent films – *Age of Extinction* (2014) and *The Last Knight* (2017) are both pretty bad. There's very little to recommend in *Age of Extinction*, outside of keeping the events in Chicago firmly in mind and seeing Optimus Prime roll out after he's repaired. It repeats the problem of revealing past Transformers involvement with Earth, this time by showing that Transformers caused the dinosaurs' extinction. It also repeats the trope of humans working with the Decepticons. Three such examples of this was more than enough. Then you have Optimus Prime simply *knowing* where the Dinobots are located, which is outside of a major Chinese city, yet no one has noticed them before. What can you say about a movie that has a character look into the air at a ship falling on him and shout to accentuate the drama – and then repeats the exact same move later in the same movie?

Being a Transformers fan sometimes feels like it requires a decent amount of masochism. I had hoped the pattern would hold, and the odd-numbered movies would be better, but *The Last Knight* feels like the most Michael Bay movie ever produced: chock full of characters and ideas, none of which are even explained and most of which are quickly jettisoned for the next daft idea. Now, we see that the Transformers were involved with Merlin, who isn't a historic figure – and when people point this out, the movie has them casually dismiss the concept of expertise and of history itself. Oh, and the Transformers were *also* involved in both World Wars – including Bumblebee, who didn't arrive on Earth until the first movie! If the movie doesn't care about its own continuity, why should we? The bad use of a McGuffin in every movie continues, this time through an absurd, size-changing sword retrieved from an ancient underwater Transformers base that humans have somehow never noticed. The film's dramatic introduction of new, one-note Decepticons, most of whom are quickly killed off, in cringe-worthy. It introduces the term "Headmaster," but cuts what was to be its only actual Headmaster. Like too many of Bay's battle scenes, there's no sense of place in the climax; the movie simply cuts from one random scene to the next. What can you say about a movie in which many critics were left confused over who was the "last knight" of the title?

That said, I think *The Last Knight* is actually better than the previous film – and maybe *Revenge of the Fallen*. Yes, it's a mess, but it so willingly *embraces* its messiness that it's kind of admirable in its sheer willingness to be the most *Bay* movie possible. Anthony Hopkins is fun to watch and seems like he's enjoying himself. And whereas I really don't like a single Transformer introduced in *Age of Extinction*, I'm charmed by both Cogman and Sqweeks. In fact, Sqweeks' moment of courage, in the climax, makes me cry.

Unfortunately, while the first three movies have a proper ending, Bay's fourth and fifth ended with a cliffhanger – none bigger than the end of *The Last Knight*, in which it's clear that Unicron is buried within the Earth. This idea is borrowed from the *Transformers: Prime* cartoon, and it would presumably have been explored in the final film of Bay's second Transformers trilogy -- which was cancelled, in the wake of *The Last Knight* underperforming.

In stark contrast, 2018's prequel *Bumblebee*, directed by Travis Knight, is a wonderful movie. It subverts the sexism of Bay's first film by telling a story of a girl and her car, and Hailee Steinfeld is wonderful as Charlie Watson. Basically, everything with her, her family, and Bumblebee works at a high level and is often charming. But everything featuring the Decepticons, who (once again) work with the military, doesn't work at all – and this unfortunately includes the climax. Even the opening on Cybertron, which tries to merge G1 and Bay designs, feels perfunctory. But it's a good movie overall, and sells the magic of Transformers in a way only the first live-action movie did.

On the other hand, 2023's *Rise of the Beasts*, directed by Steven Caple Jr., might be the worst of all the Transformers films. There's almost nothing to recommend it. The film clearly wants to return to Bay's larger cast and multiple fight scenes, but the action feels like a poor imitation of Bay, with all of the bad traits but none of the charm. The film clearly spent a lot of money shooting in places like Brooklyn and Peru, including Machu Picchu itself, yet there's never a sense of place; nothing would have been lost shooting these scenes on a soundstage.

There's exactly one good scene: in the alleyway, as Noah Diaz says goodbye to his younger brother. But even there, while the movie *wants* to think it's character-driven, the characters and relationships are remarkably cardboard. While played well, the alleyway scene is basically about nothing more than "I'm leaving to do the climax, and you hope I won't die." Although we're *told* particulars, such as their poverty or the brother having sickle cell disease, these feel like facts on file cards; none of it really affects the plot, which is asinine.

At one point, the villains use a device to build a Cybertronian base at Machu Picchu, which seems to build a massive structure out of nothing. I'm willing to pardon this. But why does a base built for Cybertronians feature human-sized ducts, which include an air duct-like opening in the middle of a random rock that looks cheap?

And if you think finding Grimlock lying around China is bad, wait until you see a secret passageway in a temple that's easy to access but which no one has before – and which leads to a cave with an opening, which also has never been found before.

Then there's Bumblebee's death, which we instantly know will be reversed. His body *happens* to be placed on a supposedly naturally occurring rock, which *happens* to be rectangular and fit him exactly. It's glowing with energon-infused rocks, which we've never seen before and which look like a cheap 1980s movie. We're told only a powerful pulse of energy would revive him, which ensures we'll get one in the climax, but doesn't explain why they'd bother to put him there. Once revived, Bumblebee joins the battle in the worst, most groan-worthy way possible, suddenly never missing a shot despite falling from a plane and shooting distant moving targets – because the music's playing, and it's supposed to be *badass*.

Then you have Pete Davidson's painfully annoying performance as Mirage, whom the movie inexplicably chooses to be its main Transformer character. In the climax, he apparently dies – which I'd at least admire, except that it's shot terribly, with his body lying over Noah's and somehow 100% covering Noah while being constantly shot yet never crushing the human. Then Mirage inexplicably turns into an exosuit (Can all Transformers do this?), which Noah uses with ninja-like expertise – because the movie wants another forced badass scene, despite having already taken pains to show us that Noah doesn't know how to use Cybertronian technology, when Mirage (it's implied) turns his dick into a gun. Although the film focuses on Davidson's grating performance, the brilliant Michelle Yeoh is utterly wasted as Airazor, while Ron Perlman isn't given much to do as Optimus Primal.

Even the revelation that Noah is asked to join G.I. Joe leaves me cold. It makes me want to see that movie instead – preferably with Noah not in it.

As of this writing, 2024's animated *Transformers One* has yet to be released. The trailers look like they've tried to turn a brutal war story into a Pixar movie, but I can still hope for the best – even as I worry that might be an expression of masochism.[*]

---

[*] First serialized on Sequart Organization's website in June 2014 and was updated for this volume.

James Roberts, Transformers Sociologist

Most other comics characters' best creators are usually well-known names for their work on other titles. Even characters who have been avoided by the most famous creators have well-known names attached. For example, Thor's most celebrated run was written and illustrated by Walter Simonson, one of American comics' most well-known artists, and was later written by Jason Aaron. Licensed comics used to be thought the least desirable assignments, as can be observed by the early history of the Transformers at Marvel. But other licensed properties have had their share of creators beloved by the wider comics world. When we think of Conan comics, for example, we might think of Barry Windsor-Smith, Roy Thomas, John Buscema, and Kurt Busiek. Even Doctor Who, whose comics were essentially limited to Britain for years, featured work by Alan Moore, Grant Morrison, Dave Gibbons, and John Ridgway. Comparatively, Transformers comics feel compartmentalized.

When it comes to Transformers writers, there are only two who have been mentioned since the heyday of Generation 1: Bob Budiansky, who wrote most of the original American comic book, and Simon Furman, who wrote most of the British comic book and the final few years of the American one, including *Generation 2*.

For decades, most fans championed Furman. Partly, this was because Budiansky's final issues were bad, leaving a bad final impression – even by his own admission, he was tiring of the comic and the demands of writing stories for new toys. This positioned his successor, Simon Furman, as a kind of savior, and Furman certainly infused the title with new energy, embracing some of the animated movie characters and the Transformers' deeper mythology.

But I also believe Furman benefitted by the fact that more people read Budiansky's American work than Furman's British work. Many fans, like me, loved the Transformers and wished they were a bit better written. When British work was reprinting, the best stories were reprinted first, and many rank Furman's *Target: 2006*, featuring the animated movie characters, as the best Transformers story ever told. On top of this, the British stories weren't available in the states for many years, adding to their mystique. Was there a huge body of work as strong as *Target: 2006*?

No, there really wasn't. The British stories had their own flaws and foibles, and for my part, more of Budiansky's stories have stuck with me through the years. But when the Transformers comics were revived, first at Dreamwave and then at IDW, it was Furman who was invited to return – to somewhat mixed reviews.

Enter James Roberts, a British Transformers fan who was active in British Transformers fandom, for which he authored fan fiction – including the long novel entitled *Eugenesis*, which he published on the final day of 2000. Set in the British comics continuity (which incorporates the U.S. comics, along with the British material), the novel expands the Transformers story to one possible conclusion. Inspired by Furman's darker stories and dramatizing the horrors of a generational war, the novel is known for being brutal, for killing off characters, and for characters committing suicide. For Roberts, the body horror wasn't gratuitous, but rather a reflection of how hard it was to kill a Transformer. It took him four years to write, and it's certainly the most wildly ambitious Transformers novel ever produced.

In 2007, Nick Roche, who had also been active in British Transformers fan circles and who was writing for IDW, involved Roberts in pitching an issue to IDW, but IDW rejected it. For 2009's *All Hail Megatron* #15, Roche used Roberts as a sounding board for the script and (although Roberts didn't work on the actual script) made sure Roberts got mentioned in the credit. On 2010's celebrated mini-series *Last Stand of the Wreckers*, Roche was struggling with his workload and brought in Roberts as co-writer.

Last Stand of the Wreckers (#1-5, Jan-May 2010) is often listed as one of the best Transformers stories ever told. It's perhaps a bit too continuity-heavy for me to do so, but it's good – and certainly wound up being a watershed event in Transformers comics.

Some of the most celebrated Transformers stories have not only been violent but exploited the differences between Transformers' and organic physiology. (See, for example, Bob Budiansky's "The Smelting Pool!" in Marvel's *Transformers* #17, June 1986). Right off the bat, *Last Stand of the Wreckers* sets the tone, as the psychopathic Decepticon Overlord (whose toy debuted only in Japan in 1988 and who was relatively unknown to American readers), during a riot at an Autobot prison on the planet Garrus-9. He tosses the prison warden, IDW continuity's version of Fortress Maximus, to the rioting crowd, who apparently rip the popular Autobot to bits.

The story follows the Wreckers, a special team of Autobots (and their human companion) who don't follow orders well, are known for taking near-impossible missions, and are the toughest warriors, embracing their potential deaths in combat. They're like the Autobot equivalent of DC's Suicide Squad, in turn influenced by Akira Kurosawa's *The Seven Samurai* (1954) and John Sturges's *The Magnificent Seven* (1960). Led by IDW's version of Ultra Magnus, the Wreckers land on Garrus-9, encountering strong resistance. During the brutal battle with the inmates, the Wreckers struggle with PTSD-style responses, find Fortress Maximus's mutilated body, find a computer that judges Transfomers by determining their internal sense of guilt (echoing the *Red Dwarf* episode "Justice"), only get past it by one of the Wreckers willingly sacrificing himself, and discover that Overlord has already killed every Autobot prisoner, and brutally kill a whole lot of Decepticons. In the end, Prowl (best known as one of the original G1 Autobots) is shown to be a kind of spymaster, who is more than comfortable deceiving Autobots and sending them to their deaths for the greater good.

It's dark stuff.

After a few projects that never saw print, Roberts pitched a Megatron origin story, which ultimately became the two-issue "Chaos Theory," appearing in *Transformers* #22-23 (July-August 2011) and illustrated by celebrated Transformers artist Alex Milne. The story suffers from being part of an ongoing storyline, in which Megatron had recently surrendered. As such, the present-day material has Optimus Prime struggling with what to do with the Decepticon. There's a subplot about what the Matrix can do and why it hurt Optimus when he got it, which isn't resolved here. Also,

Optimus Prime loses his cool and briefly tortures Megatron – in fact, we find out that another Autobot cut the power out of fear the violence would kill Megatron.

It's the flashbacks, set before the Transformers' civil war, that are most remembered about the story. There, Megatron is depicted as a political dissident, while Orion Pax, the future Optimus Prime, essentially acts as a local chief of police. When we meet Megatron, he's being brutalized by the police force, prominently including Whirl (a future Autobot). Orion Pax intervenes and welcomes Megatron's ideas, even if Optimus doesn't agree with all of them. Later, a terrorist attack escalates tensions, and Orion Pax refuses to let Whirl off for his crimes (essentially refusing to participate in the "blue wall" of real-life police forces), and Pax becomes convinced the planet's Senate is corrupt. It's a startling redefinition of the genesis of the civil war, which was originally depicted as simply the result of Megatron's quest for power. While that had been complicated previously (e.g. in Dreamwave's *The War Within* mini-series), Megatron's cause had never been so sympathetic.

In fact, Roberts essentially goes further, converting Orion Pax to Megatron's cause. Pax interrupts the Senate, then currently debating whether to crack down on civil liberties in the wake of terrorism (echoing real-world post-9/11 debates), and delivers a speech before he's dragged out. He voices the dissidents' concerns, pointing out that plenty don't wish to perform the functions for which they were designed – essentially, their vehicle modes determine their caste status. It's a powerful study of the implications implicit in the original concept of the Transformers (and which obsessed me as a kid in the 1980s): that some Transformers were designed to be cars and others military vehicles. Roberts shows us the sociological consequences of such divisions – again, not for the first time in Transfomers lore, but in a more forceful way than before.

In his speech, Pax gives a new, in-continuity explanation for the term "Autobot." It's not short of "automotive" at all. Rather, it's used in derision for those in power, since they're "automotons." Pax then embraces the term and redefines it as short for "autonomous." Pax then delivers the three questions Megatron had for the Senate, letting himself become the famous villain's mouthpiece.

While strongly influential, it's the flashback material that really shines. Examined as a Transformers story, the continuing story is simply too prominent for the story to even make sense on its own. Its title, "Chaos Theory," even reflects the storyline it led into, which was titled simply "Chaos." Co-written by regular series writer Mike Costa and James Roberts, "Chaos" saw the IDW version of Galvatron and his minions (no longer changed versions of other characters) attack Cybertron. The storyline ran in even-numbered issues, with a separate story (not co-written by Roberts) set on Earth running in odd-numbered issues. The series ended with issue #31 (Dec 2011). Although it can honestly be hard to tell from actually reading the stories (which seem no more climactic than plenty of other tales), their key conceit is the end, once and for all, of the Autobot-Decepticon war.

It was a bold, new direction for the franchise, which had been defined by that conflict. IDW had previously shifted its ongoing Transformers story with *All Hail Megatron*, which essentially asked, "What if Megatron won and conquered the Earth?" Now, IDW had decided on an even bolder move, asking, "What would the Transformers be like, if their war finally ended?"

Roberts co-wrote, with John Barber, the special launching this new era, titled *The Death of Optimus Prime* (Dec 2011) and illustrated by Nick Roche. Lest you be confused by the special's title, Optimus Prime doesn't die – instead, seeing that he's a polarizing figure defined by the long, now-ended war, he leaves, calling himself Orion Pax again. The special set up the two new, ongoing Transformers titles. One, set of Cybertron, would follow the attempts to rebuild and to manage diverse political interests, while various characters jockey for power. The other – written by Roberts, largely illustrated by Roche, and subtitled *More than Meets the Eye* – would follow Rodimus and a crew of former Autobots and Decepticons aboard the Lost Light as they search for the legendary "Knights of Cybertron," which may or may not exist.

This might seem like *More than Meets the Eye* is the marginal side title. But despite the praise heaped on *Last Stand of the Wreckers* and "Chaos Theory," it's *More than Meets the Eye* for which Roberts is most praised. Right from the start, the tone and style that we'd identify with James Roberts' later work is present in full force. In retrospect, it makes earlier Roberts scripts feel compromised, as if he were too bound by others' plot points to express his own voice.

One key ingredient, missing from earlier efforts, is humor: Roberts routinely has characters misunderstand each other, speak sarcastically under their breath, or offer side comments that don't advance the plot and that sometimes even clog the panels with word balloons. But it mostly works, and it feels like you're reading dialogue intended to be read aloud. The flow captures something of the feel of a character-dominated TV show, making conventional comics feel stilted in comparison.

On the one hand, you could call Roberts' work a Transformers sitcom. The characters' personalities, often expressed through downtime, feels more nuanced and idiosyncratic than ever before, and their storylines take dozens of issues to play out. They hang out at Swerve's bar as if it were Cheers. They watch TV, listen to music, drink, and fall in love – all the trivial things we associate with being human. While there's action, the characters rarely actually *transform* or use their vehicle modes. And gone are the human characters too many writers use as audience identification tools. His stories are about robot personalities, playing off of one another, working through their issues over time.

The central conceit of *More than Meets the Eye* seems designed for this emphasis, with the diverse cast stuck on a ship together, working through their past allegiances and traumas. In fact, one of the characters Roberts invented is a psychiatrist named Rung – whose (evil, it turns out) rival is named Froid. Rodimus is out of his depth, Ultra Magnus is uptight, Whirl committed terrible crimes in the past, and Cyclonus wants revenge – but all evolve beyond these motivations, showing that even robots defined by war can grow and change.

Despite this very character-driven approach, which seems to emphasize the Transformers' *humanity*, Roberts stubbornly never forgets that these are *not* biological human characters. Key to the violence that defined his early Transformers work (and even the

1986 animated movie) is the central observation that Transformers can take a lot of punishment. You can demolish them and torture them, and they'll feel the pain – but they can still be rebuilt. Their anatomy is simply different. Roberts takes this observation further than ever before.

After all, when they don't reproduce sexually, why would the Transformers be bothered by couplings we'd identify as homosexual? Gender has always been a complicated issue with the Transformers. But if most present as male, wouldn't they fall in love? And so we're treated to an understanding of different types of bonds in Transformers culture, like different types of marriages – which merges Roberts's character-driven approach with his focus on how the Transformers are almost unfathomably, biologically *different*. Above all, there's the love story of Chromedome and Rewind – an odd couple, if ever there were one, but one that Roberts manages to sell from start to finish. (To its credit, Hasbro supported the depiction.) It's no coincidence that many trans and non-binary fans have repeatedly expressed that Roberts gave them a voice for the first time in Transformers history – something that, to his credit, clearly matters to the writer.

And while Roberts doesn't often have his characters *transform*, what they transform *into* is of paramount importance. To be fair, this emphasis didn't originate with Roberts: it goes back to the simple observation that the original Autobots turned into cars and trucks, while the original Decepticons turned into military vehicles and weapons – along with, for some reason, micro-cassette tapes. The depiction of the civil war on Cybertron, in Marvel's *Transformers* #1, had my childhood brain creating its own headcanon, in which that war came down to a military coup: it seemed only natural that the robots who turned into military vehicles, seeing themselves as stronger, would seek to take over. IDW's previous writers – to whom, it's only fair to note, Roberts contributed – had pushed this a bit further, but it was Roberts that let these ideas flower into the schools of thought that dominated Transformers society. Key to Transformers history was *functionalism*: the idea that one's alt mode determined one's function in society – the mechanical equivalent of biology being destiny. In fact, one of the longstanding mysteries of the series is what Rung's alt mode is. The Transformers may have been free of race and gender, as we understand it, but they still had discrimination based on alt mode. To his credit, Roberts never uses this simply as a one-to-one surrogate for racism or sexism; instead, he tries to imagine how this different biology (for lack of a better word) would play itself out over time.

Central to Roberts' take on the Transformers is that they're not biologically human. He doesn't seem interested in telling stories that could be told in other franchises, with other characters. Consider the two-part story focusing on Ratchet, in issues #4-5 (April-May 2012). One of my problems with the Transformers, in the past, was that the need for more toys caused characters to be duplicated: after having characterized Ratchet, did the Autobots need another medic who transformed into an ambulance with First Aid? The answer, of course, is *yes*, because there were new toys to tell. Roberts manages to differentiate them right from the start, infusing their culture with tropes from medical stories. In Roberts's story, Ratchet is on the Lost Light. In something of a cliché from hospital shows (where surgeons might struggle with a nervous tick, for example), Ratchet's hands are wearing out, and his days as a medic are numbered. He travels to a medical outpost, where First Aid works and which is run by another medic named Pharma. Life there feels like something out of *M.A.S.H.* only darker, with medics having to make harsh choices and competing with their mentors. The team from Lost Light finds that a plague has struck the facility, leading to some zombie action. We eventually find out that Pharma's been killing patients to bribe the Decepticons with the parts of the dead – something analogous to the organ trade but still taking advantage of how robot medics aren't exactly like human ones. It's a hard-edged war story rooted in Transformers biology. In the climax, Pharma hangs off the facility's roof and falls after getting his hands chopped off – which, in a horrific touch, still cling to the roof. After administering the cure, we find that Ratchet has replaced his failing hands with those of the legendary Pharma – a nice touch which would have been impossible in any non-robot story.

That story also features the Decepticon Justice Division – a group of brutal Decepticons, led by Tarn, who torture and punish Decepticon traitors. Tarn memorably wears a Decepticon logo for a face, and one of his underlings transforms into an electric chair. They're set up as the ultimate boogeymen, feared by Autobots but even more feared by Decepticons, many of whom never enjoyed fighting but understood the penalties for failing to do so. Along with Rung, the D.J.C. were some of the most celebrated characters from Roberts's run, and Tarn especially has had a life beyond it.

Running for about five years, *More than Meets the Eye* was largely illustrated by Alex Milne. It was hampered slightly by having to cross over with the "main" title – which didn't make a lot of sense, given that the Lost Light was thought to be destroyed and on a separate mission – for the "Dark Cybertron" event (2013-2014). But Roberts made the most of this, adjusting his cast by adding Megatron himself. A mass murderer feared by countless planets over a timescale unimaginable to human minds, Megatron now professed to be a pacifist. His redemption and conversion to the Autobot cause would be one of Roberts's greatest storylines – especially given how tempting his return to evil would have been. In fact, Megatron would play a key role in the defeat of the D.J.C., near the end of *More than Meets the Eye*.

After 57 issues and an annual, *More than Meets the Eye* came to an end during one of IDW's periodic relaunches of the Transformers titles, now being retooled by the *Revolution* crossover as part of a larger Hasbro universe. Roberts was given the opportunity to continue the story with a new series, subtitled *Lost Light*, which ran for 25 more issues, largely illustrated by Jack Lawrence. In 2018, IDW then ended the longest-running Transformers comic continuity, which it had begun in 2005, in favor of a new story showing the origins of the Transformers' civil war. Ironically, it was terrain Roberts had helped to pave with "Chaos Theory," which would remain more fondly remembered than the new continuity's version. Short-sighted though this may have been, Roberts was at least permitted to send off his characters, in *Lost Light* #25 (Oct 2018). Rodimus, now with Megatron as co-captain, took the ship into a new universe, potentially continuing their adventures forever.

In retrospect, Roberts's work – especially *More than Meets the*

Eye, with Alex Milne – is often cited as the best set of Transformers stories ever produced. But Transformers fandom is incredibly fractured, and his work isn't to everyone's taste. Some object that it's too tied to past continuity, which is inevitable when it is one series among two or more, which themselves continued over six years of previous stories. Others object to the soap operatic qualities – either because this goes against the grain of robots at war or because it's too human-esque. No doubt, Roberts's work exhibits a tension between his strongly focus on the Transformers as robots, with their own cultures and with stories that can't be told in other franchises, and their very human relationships. Every once in a while, I catch a pun amid the banter and the fact that everyone's speaking English and acting very human punctuates the illusion. I grew up with Bob Budiansky and Simon Furman, and I personally like episodic stories that, while they might be part of larger continuities, can be shared with anyone without much prior knowledge. Because of this, it's harder to point to a single issue or story written by Roberts, the way one might with Budiansky or Furman.

But if fandom is divided, the majority seem to want Roberts to return and adore what he accomplished. There can be little doubt that Roberts brought an intelligence and long-term narrative maturity to Transformers stories that they had never seen before. His mythology and backstory was deeper than the Transformers had ever seen. It's no coincidence that this maturity combined with a focus on inclusivity, even without a human cast, that the franchise had too long lacked. His characters were deep enough to make adults cry. Many have cast a long shadow over subsequent incarnations of the franchise.

In the history of Transformers comics writers, there have been three greats. Two were there at the beginning. James Roberts alone has been able to carve out that status for himself, despite coming decades later. May the light he shed on the franchise and its possibilities not go ignored, forgotten, or lost.[*]

---

[*] This essay is new to this volume.

About the Author

In 1996, while still an undergraduate, Dr. Julian Darius founded what would become Sequart Organization, which promotes comics and popular culture as legitimate forms of art. In 2005, Darius published the first scholarly book on Christopher Nolan's Batman films. In 2015, he released *Classics on Infinite Earths*, a massive study of the Justice League and DC's shared universe. He has also published books on (among other subjects) *Batman: The Killing Joke*, which elaborated a theory on the book's plot that was praised by Kevin Smith and Grant Morrison; Jack Kirby's comic-book continuation of *2001: A Space Odyssey*; and *Mai, the Psychic Girl*. He has also produced several documentaries about comics for the organization.

In 2011, Darius founded Martian Lit, which publishes creative work, including his novel *Nira/Sussa*, his screenplay *Watching People Burn*, and his Martian Universe set of interlocking comics covering 20,000 years of Martian history.

Darius co-hosts, with Scott Weatherly, the Stories out of Time and Space podcast on sci-fi movies and television.

After graduating magna cum laude from Lawrence University (Appleton, Wisconsin), Darius obtained his M.A. in English, authoring a thesis on John Milton and utopianism. In 2002, he moved to Waikiki, teaching college while obtaining an M.A. in French (high honors) and a Ph.D. in English.

He currently lives in Hawaii, where he teaches writing.

Also from Sequart

Books on Comics Characters:

Gods and Marvels: Essays on Moon Knight
Judging Dredd: Examining the World of Judge Dredd
From Bayou to Abyss: Examining John Constantine, Hellblazer
Moving Target: The History and Evolution of Green Arrow
Teenagers from the Future: Essays on the Legion of Super-Heroes
The Devil is in the Details: Examining Matt Murdock and Daredevil

Books on Grant Morrison:

Grant Morrison: The Early Years
Our Sentence is Up: Seeing Grant Morrison's *The Invisibles*
Curing the Postmodern Blues: Reading Grant Morrison and Chris
      Weston's *The Filth* in the 21st Century
The Anatomy of Zur-en-Arrh: Understanding Grant Morrison's
      Batman

Books on Warren Ellis:

Shot in the Face: A Savage Journey to the Heart of
      Transmetropolitan
Keeping the World Strange: A *Planetary* Guide
Voyage in Noise: Warren Ellis and the Demise of Western
      Civilization
Warren Ellis: The Captured Ghosts Interviews

Books on Sci-Fi Franchises:

Unauthorized Offworld Activation: Exploring the Stargate Franchise
Somewhere Beyond the Heavens: Exploring Battlestar Galactica
The Cyberpunk Nexus: Exploring the Blade Runner Universe
The Sacred Scrolls: Comics on the Planet of the Apes
Bright Lights, Ape City: Examining the Planet of the Apes Mythos
New Life and New Civilizations: Exploring Star Trek Comics
A Long Time Ago: Exploring the Star Wars Cinematic Universe
A Galaxy Far, Far Away: Exploring Star Wars Comics
A More Civilized Age: Exploring the Star Wars Expanded Universe

The Weirdest Sci-Fi Comic Ever Made: Understanding Jack Kirby's
 2001: A Space Odyssey

Books on TV and Movies:

Improving the Foundations: *Batman Begins* from Comics to Screen

Why Do We Fall?: Examining Christopher Nolan's *The Dark Knight
 Trilogy*

Mutant Cinema: The X-Men Trilogy from Comics to Screen

Gotham City 14 Miles: 14 Essays on Why the 1960s Batman TV
 Series Matters

Time is a Flat Circle: Examining *True Detective*, Season One

Other Books:

The British Invasion: Alan Moore, Neil Gaiman, Grant Morrison, and
 the Invention of the Modern Comic Book Writer

How to Analyze & Review Comics: A Handbook on Comics Criticism

Moving Panels: Translating Comics to Film

Humans and Paragons: Essays on Super-Hero Justice

Musings on Monsters: Observations on the World of Classic Horror

Classics on Infinite Earths: The Justice League and DC Crossover
 Canon

The Mignolaverse: Hellboy and the Comics Art of Mike Mignola

The Best There is at What He Does: Examining Chris Claremont's X-
 Men

And the Universe so Big: Understanding *Batman: The Killing Joke*

Minutes to Midnight: Twelve Essays on *Watchmen*

When Manga Came to America: Super-Hero Revisionism in *Mai, the
 Psychic Girl*

The Future of Comics, The Future of Men: Matt Fraction's *Casanova*

Documentary Films:

Diagram for Delinquents

She Makes Comics

The Image Revolution

Neil Gaiman: Dream Dangerously

Grant Morrison: Talking with Gods

Warren Ellis: Captured Ghosts

Comics in Focus: Chris Claremont's X-Men

For more information and for exclusive content,
visit Sequart.org.

www.ingramcontent.com/pod-product-compliance
Lightning Source LLC
LaVergne TN
LVHW052027080426
835513LV00018B/2206

9781940589350